The Great Counted Cross-Stitch Book

Ed & Stevie Baldwin

This book is dedicated with love to
John and Annabelle Thompson

The Great Counted Cross-Stitch Book

Ed & Stevie Baldwin

Created by The Family Workshop, Inc.

Editorial Director: Janet Weberling
Art Director: Dale Crain
Photography: Bill Welch
Project Designs: April Bail and Stevie Baldwin;
                except pages 43, 47, and 66, Melinda Gorney
Production: Christopher Berg, Deborah Howell, Barbara McMahon,
           Jacqueline Nelson, Kim Pula, Roberta Taff, and
           Wanda Young

For Western Publishing Company, Inc.

Jonathan P. Latimer, Editorial Director, Adult Books
Susan A. Roth, Senior Editor
Karen Stray Nolting, Copy Editor

Published by: Western Publishing Company, Inc.
                 850 Third Avenue
                 New York, New York 10022

ISBN: 0-307-42027-2 (SOFT), 0-307-42028-0 (HARD)
Library of Congress Catalog Card Number: 82-84290
© 1983 The Family Workshop, Inc. Printed in U.S.A.

Special thanks to the following crafters:
Sharon Austin, Holly Bail, Rachel Bail, Phyllis Barnes, Jamie Booker, Judy Gahm, Melinda Gorney, Jill Hodgdon, Deborah Howell, Pat Huendhal, Jeannette Hurst, Judy Jordan, Deborah Lincoln, Barbara McMahon, Mary Morse, D.J. Olin, Roberta Parenti, Charlotte Reheard, Janis Schemet, Roberta Taff, and Wanda Young

Additional craft patterns are available from The Family Workshop, Inc. For a catalog, send $1.50 to: The Family Workshop, Department 10018, P. O. Box 159, Bixby, Oklahoma, 74008.

Table of Contents

Making the body

Note: All seams are ½ inch unless otherwise specified.

1. Scale drawings for the sewing patterns are provided in **Figure B**. Enlarge the drawings to full-size paper patterns, and cut the following muslin pieces: one crown, one face, one chest, two bodies, four arms, and four legs.

2. Center the cross-stitched facial features over the muslin face and mark the center point of the nose on the muslin. Sew the rounded shank button to the muslin at this point. Reposition the aida cloth over the muslin, placing the wrong side of the aida against the muslin, and baste the fabrics together close to the edge. The button will make Becky's nose stand out slightly.

1 square = 1 inch

Figure B

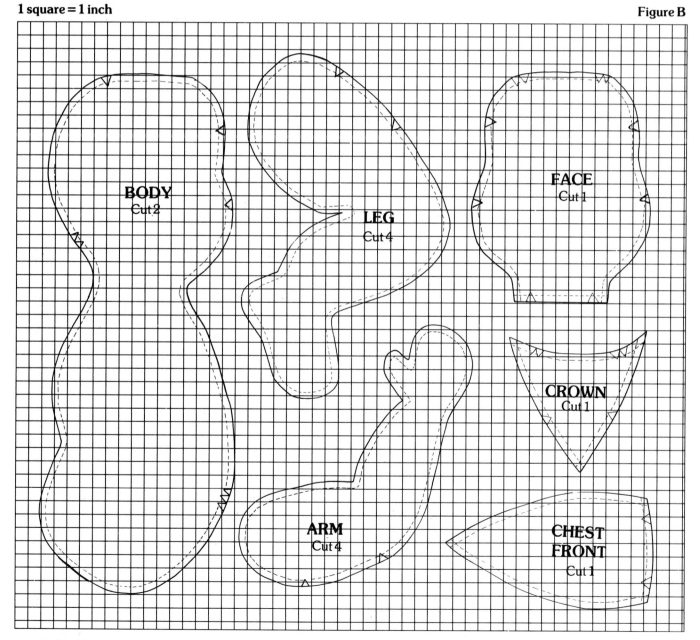

Figure C

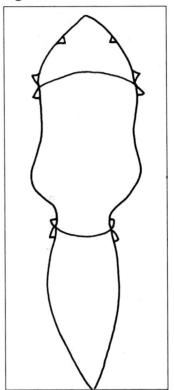

Figure D

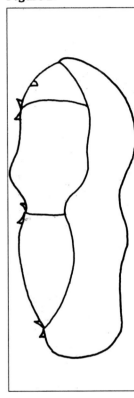

3. Pin the crown to the upper edge of the face piece, placing right sides together and easing the curve between the matching double notches. Since the aida cloth face will be in between the muslin pieces, you may have to hold them up to a light to see the notches. Stitch the seam, clip the curve, and press open.

4. Pin the chest piece to the neck edge of the face, placing right sides together and matching notches. Stitch the seam and press it open (**Figure C**).

5. Pin one muslin body piece along one side of the crown/face/chest assembly, placing right sides together and matching the notches and curves. Stitch the seam from the point of the crown to the lower edge of the chest, clip the curves, and press the seam (**Figure D**). Sew the remaining muslin body piece to the opposite side.

6. Fold the assembled body in half lengthwise, right sides together, and stitch the seam along the raw edges of the body pieces. Leave the seam unstitched between the single and double notches at the back of the head. Clip the curves and turn the body right side out through the opening.

7. Stuff the body with fiberfill and then whipstitch the opening together using heavy duty thread. If you want your doll to have a more distinct dividing line between the head and neck, work a line of basting stitches across the top of the neck, from side to side. Pull the stitches tight to form the lower head contour.

8. To make an arm, pin two muslin arm pieces right sides together and stitch the seam all the way around the edge, leaving it open between the notches. Clip the curves, turn the arm right side out, and stuff. Whipstitch the opening together, using heavy duty thread. Repeat this step using the remaining two muslin arm pieces.

9. To make the legs, stitch, turn, and stuff the muslin leg pieces, following the procedures for making the arms.

10. Place an assembled arm on each side of the body at the shoulder line. Be sure that you have the correct arm on each side – thumbs should be pointing upward. Using a long needle and heavy-duty thread, stitch through one arm, push the needle all the way through the body, and on through the arm at the opposite side (**Figure E**). Repeat this procedure several times, going back and forth through the arms and body until the joints are secure.

11. Follow the same procedure to attach the legs to opposite sides of the lower body (**Figure F**).

Figure E

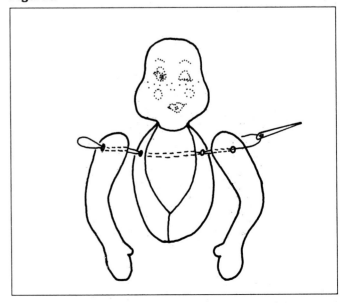

Kids' Stuff

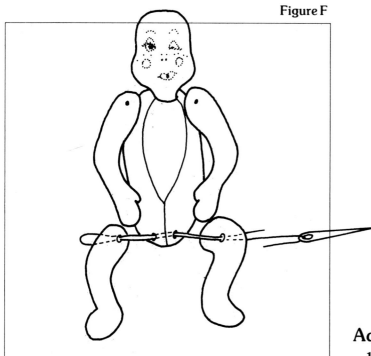

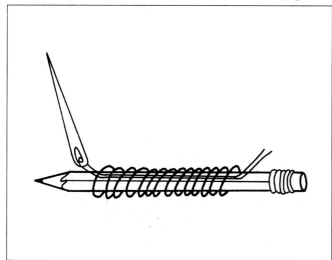

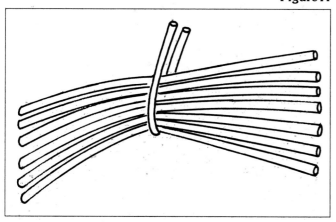

Adding the hair

1. To make Becky's curls, you will be working with a continuous length of pale yellow rug yarn, heavy-duty thread, and a sharp needle. Begin by stitching through one end of the yarn to attach it securely to the head. (You may start at any point on the head – it really doesn't matter where.) Don't cut the thread; just leave the needle where you can easily find it again.

2. Place a fat pencil (or other long, roundish object) next to the head at the point where the yarn is attached. Wrap the yarn loosely around the pencil about twenty times. Now take up the needle again, insert it between the loops of yarn and the pencil at one end (**Figure G**), and pull it out through the opposite end.

3. Carefully remove the pencil, compressing the curl, and take another stitch into the head to secure the curl in place. Repeat this procedure to make closely-spaced curls all over the head. When your thread runs low, lock the stitch and re-thread your needle. When you come to the end of the yarn, tie on the next skein and continue to work, tucking the tied ends underneath a curl. At the end of the last curl, stitch the yarn end securely to the head underneath the curl.

4. For each ponytail, cut a handful of 16-inch-long strands of yarn and tie them together at the center using a short length of yarn (**Figure H**). Fold them in half, smooth them down, and tie the ponytail securely to one or two curls on one side of the head. Cut a length of pink ribbon and tie a bow around the ponytail near the head. Repeat this procedure to make the second ponytail.

Making the dress

1. You'll find scale drawings for all of the clothing patterns in **Figure I**. Enlarge the drawings to full-size paper patterns. Pay careful attention to the "place on fold" notations, and cut the following pieces from pink-and-white gingham: one dress front, two dress backs, one front yoke, two back yokes, two sleeves, and two back plackets.

Figure I

1 square = 1 inch

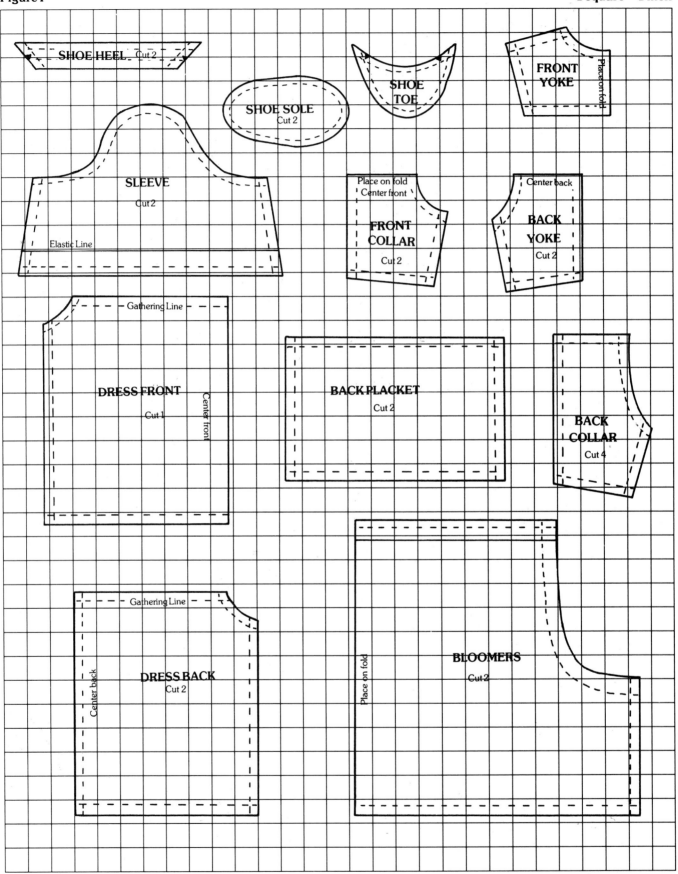

SHOE HEEL Cut 2

SHOE SOLE Cut 2

SHOE TOE

FRONT YOKE

Place on fold

SLEEVE Cut 2

Elastic Line

Place on fold
Center front

FRONT COLLAR Cut 2

Center back

BACK YOKE Cut 2

Gathering Line

DRESS FRONT Cut 1

Center front

BACK PLACKET Cut 2

BACK COLLAR Cut 4

Gathering Line

Center back

DRESS BACK Cut 2

Place on fold

BLOOMERS Cut 2

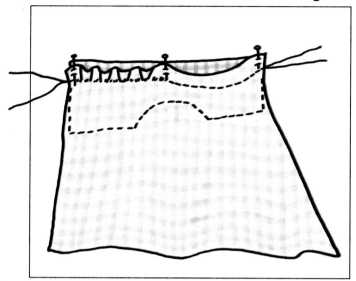

Figure J

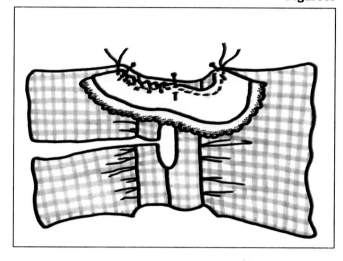

Figure K

Figure L

Figure M

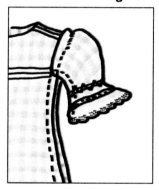

Figure N

2. Run a line of basting stitches near the upper edge of the dress front piece, just inside the seam allowance. Pin the dress front piece to the front yoke piece, right sides together, pulling up the basting stitches to form even gathers (**Figure J**). Stitch the seam and press it open.

3. Follow the same procedures to attach each dress back piece to a back yoke piece.

4. Place the front and back dress assemblies right sides together, stitch the shoulder seams, and press them open.

5. On the straight lower edge of each sleeve piece, press a ¼-inch hem allowance to the wrong side and add a length of 1-inch-wide eyelet trim. Run a line of basting stitches along the curved upper edge, just inside the seam line.

6. With right sides together, pin the curved edge of one sleeve to the armhole edge on one side of the dress, pulling up the basting stitches to form even gathers (**Figure K**). Stitch the seam and press the allowance toward the sleeve. Repeat this procedure to attach the remaining sleeve to the opposite side of the dress.

7. Measure around Becky's arm just above the elbow, and cut two lengths of elastic, each slightly longer than the arm measurement. Use a zig-zag machine setting to stitch one piece of elastic to the wrong side of each sleeve, approximately 1 inch from the lower edge, stretching the elastic as you go (**Figure L**).

8. Fold the dress right sides together, and stitch the underarm and side seam on each side (**Figure M**).

9. Fold one back placket piece in half lengthwise, wrong sides together. Place the folded placket along one side of the dress back opening, on the right side of the fabric with raw edges even (**Figure N**). Stitch the seam, press the placket toward the opening, and the seam allowance toward the dress. Repeat this step to attach the remaining placket to the opposite side of the opening.

Figure O

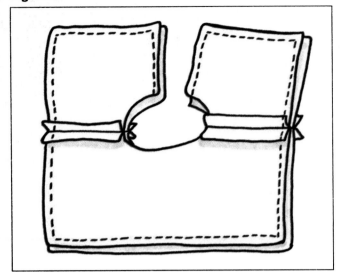

Figure Q

Figure P

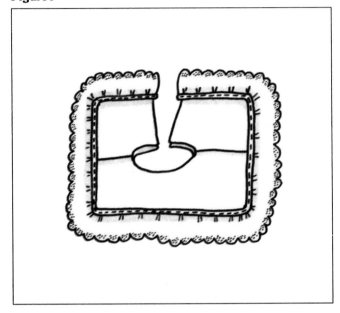

Adding the collar

1. Cut two front collar pieces and four back collar pieces from white seersucker. (Note "place on fold" for the front collar pieces.)

2. To make the collar, stitch two back collar pieces to one front collar piece at the shoulder seams placing right sides together. Open the collar and press the seams open. To make the collar facing, repeat this step using the remaining pieces.

3. Place the collar and facing right sides together and stitch a continuous seam around all straight edges, leaving the neckline open and unstitched (**Figure O**). Trim the seam allowance at the corners, and turn the assembled collar right side out.

4. Stitch a length of the widest eyelet trim around the entire lower edge of the collar, starting and ending at the back opening, and leaving a short allowance of eyelet at each end (**Figure P**). Turn the allowances to the wrong side.

5. Pin the collar to the dress around the neck edges, placing the right side of the collar against the wrong side of the dress fabric, and matching shoulder seams. (The back opening edges of the collar will not quite reach to the back opening edges of the plackets.) Stitch a ⅝-inch seam around the neck edge. Clip the curve in several places and clip the back plackets from the neckline edge down to the seam line at the points where the collar ends (**Figure Q**).

6. Turn the collar to the right side of the dress and press. Turn the clipped edges of the plackets to the wrong side and press. Topstitch through all thicknesses, ¼ inch from the turned neckline edge. Stitch a length of narrow eyelet trim around the right side of the neckline, so that the eyelet points upward. (This will cover the line of contour stitches across the aida cloth neck.)

7. Stitch a length of pink ribbon to each side of the back opening at the neckline edge. (The ribbons should be long enough to tie together in a bow and hold the neckline closed when Becky is dressed.)

8. To add the cross-stitched collar trim, turn the short raw edges of the aida cloth strip to the wrong side, so that the strip fits across the front of the collar. Hand stitch the strip in place.

9. Press a ¼-inch hem allowance to the wrong side around the lower dress edge. Stitch a length of the widest eyelet trim around the hem, turning the ends of the eyelet to the wrong side at the back opening edges.

Figure R

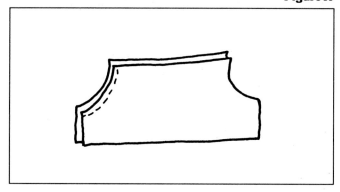

Figure S

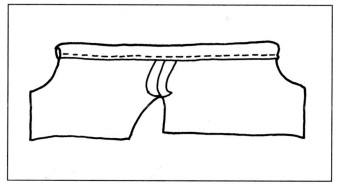

Figure T

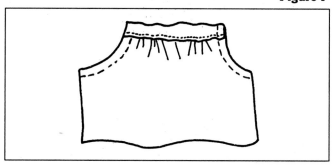

Figure U

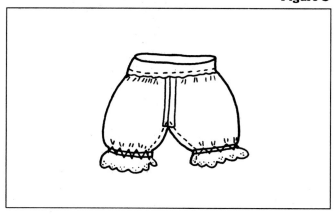

Making the bloomers

1. Cut two bloomer pieces from the gingham fabric. (Note "place on fold.") Place them right sides together and stitch the front curved seam as shown in **Figure R** (⅝-inch seam allowance). Clip the curve and press the seam.

2. Open the bloomers and press a ¼-inch hem allowance to the wrong side of the waist edge. Turn the waist edge down again along the casing line (½ inch below the turned edge), and press. Stitch through all layers to form the elastic casing as shown in **Figure S**.

3. Measure and cut a piece of elastic slightly longer than Becky's waist measurement. Thread the elastic through the casing, tacking each end to one edge of the casing to hold it in place. Fold the bloomers right sides together and stitch the curved back seam, catching the ends of the elastic in the seam (**Figure T**).

4. Press a ¼-inch hem allowance to the wrong side on each lower leg edge. Stitch a length of lace trim on the right side of the fabric along each turned edge. Measure and cut two lengths of elastic, each slightly longer than the upper leg measurement of the doll. Using a zig-zag machine setting, stitch a length of elastic 1 inch above each hemmed lower leg edge, stretching the elastic as you stitch.

5. Fold the bloomers right sides together, matching center front and back seams, and stitch the inner leg seam from one lower edge to the other (**Figure U**).

Making the shoes

1. Cut two shoe toe pieces, two heel pieces, and two sole pieces from pink cotton fabric.

2. With right sides together, stitch one short edge of the heel to one end of the lower curved edge of the toe, as shown in **Figure V**, matching notches. Fold the heel over itself, and stitch the remaining short edge to the opposite end of the curved toe edge, matching notches again.

3. Turn the assembled shoe top right side out, and stitch a length of lace trim around the upper raw edge (**Figure W**). With right sides together, stitch the upper assembly to the sole, easing the heel portion to fit.

4. Turn the shoe right side out and run a line of basting stitches around the upper edge, using heavy-duty thread. To make the ankle strap, cut an 18-inch length of pink ribbon, fold it in half, and stitch the center point inside the center back of the heel. Put the shoe on Becky's foot, pull up the basting stitches so that the upper edge fits securely, and tie the ankle straps in a bow at the front. Repeat steps 2 through 4 to create the second shoe.

Finishing touches

1. Use heavy-duty thread to take two or three stitches through each of Becky's knees (from side to side), and pull the thread tightly to create dimples. Lock the stitch and cut the thread. Brush powdered cheek blusher on the knee caps.

2. Use a sharp needle and a generous length of heavy-duty thread to soft sculpture fingers on each of Becky's hands. Follow the entry and exit points illustrated in **Figure X**.

    a. Knot the end of the thread. Enter the needle at point 1 on the palm, and exit directly opposite 1 on the back of the hand.

    b. Wrap the thread around the end of the hand, enter at 1 on the palm, push the needle under the surface and exit at 2 on the palm. Pull the thread tightly to form the first finger.

    c. Hold tension on the thread as you repeat this procedure at points 2 and 3 to create the remaining finger lines. Lock the stitch and cut the thread when you have completed one hand, and then soft sculpture the fingers on the other hand.

3. Help Becky get into her clothing. To add a little extra "character" and a well-rounded appearance, we stuffed additional fiberfill inside the back of the bloomers.

Figure V

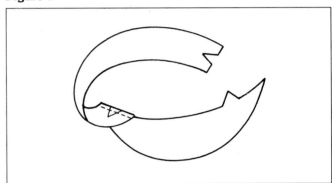

Figure W

Figure X

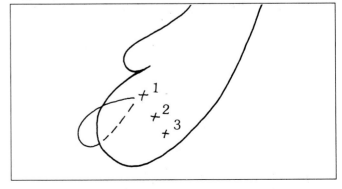

Sailboat Crib Quilt

Here's a soft, cuddly quilt that Wynken, Blynken, and Nod would definitely enjoy. The patchwork top has alternating squares of red and blue bandana-print fabrics, and squares cross-stitched with a sailboat design. It's backed with flannel.

Materials

1½ yards of 45-inch-wide red bandana-print fabric.
2 yards of 45-inch-wide blue bandana-print fabric.
Five 12-inch squares of 11-count aida cloth.
41 x 46-inch piece of white flannel.
41 x 46-inch piece of quilt batting.
5½ yards of white yarn.
Blue and red embroidery floss.
1¾ yards of blue rickrack.
Tapestry needle, white thread, needle, pins, scissors, tape measure, sewing machine, embroidery needle.

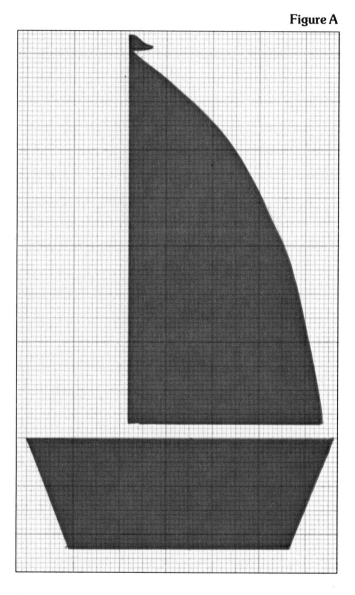

Cross-stitch

Each of the aida cloth squares is cross-stitched with the sailboat design shown in the stitching graph, **Figure A**. The graph is not color coded, since the color scheme is not intricate and all of the squares don't have the same color scheme. On four of the squares, work the sail in blue and the hull and flag in red. Reverse the colors for the remaining square.

Figure B

Figure C

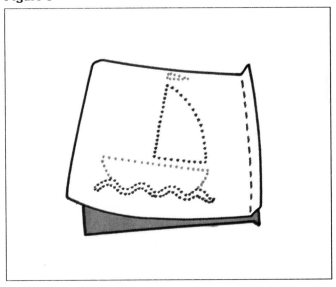

Figure D

Figure E

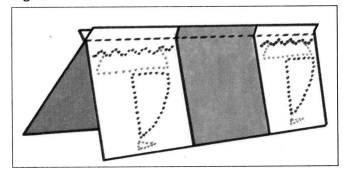

Figure F

Making the patchwork top

Note: All seam allowances are ½ inch.

1. The patchwork top consists of four fabric squares, five cross-stitched squares, and four border strips. To complete the five cross-stitched squares, first staystitch ¼ inch from all edges. Cut a 12-inch length of rickrack to serve as the waterline on each, and stitch it across the square just under the sailboat hull (**Figure B**).

2. Cut two 12-inch squares from the red bandana fabric, and two from the blue. Staystitch ¼ inch from each edge.

3. Cut two border strips from the red fabric, each 34 x 4½ inches; and two border strips from the blue fabric, each 41 x 7 inches.

4. Assemble the top patchwork row using one red bandana square and two aida cloth squares with the sails stitched in blue. Place one cross-stitched square on top of the red square, right sides together, and stitch along the right-hand edge (**Figure C**). Press the seam open.

5. Place the other cross-stitched square on top of the red square, right sides together, and stitch the left-hand seam. Press open (**Figure D**).

6. Follow the same procedures to assemble an identical bottom row of squares. For the middle row use the two blue bandana squares and the remaining aida cloth square, which was cross-stitched in a reversed color scheme.

7. To join the rows, place the middle row right side up on a flat surface. Place the top row right side down over the middle row. (As you look down at it, you should see the wrong side of the top row fabrics, and the sailboats should appear upside down.) Pin carefully, matching seams, and stitch along the upper edge (**Figure E**). Press the seam open.

8. Stitch the bottom row to the lower edge of the middle row in the same manner, and press open.

9. The border strips are added next. Place the assembled squares right side up on a flat surface. Place one red border strip right side down over them, so that one long edge of the strip is even with one edge of the patchwork (**Figure F**). Stitch the seam and press open.

Kids' Stuff

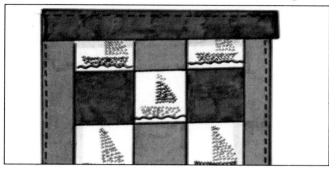

Figure I

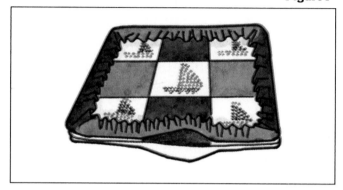

Figure J

10. Follow the same procedures to attach the remaining red strip to the opposite edge of the patchwork, and press open. Attach the two blue strips to the remaining raw edges of the patchwork and the ends of the red strips (**Figure G**).

Adding the ruffle

1. The ruffle strip is made by piecing together alternating 10-inch-wide strips of red and blue bandana fabric. Cut three strips of red fabric, each 45 x 10 inches. Cut three additional red strips, each 7 x 10 inches. Piece together one short and one long red strip, to form one strip 51 x 10 inches. (To piece, place the strips right sides together, and stitch the seam along one 10-inch edge. Press open.) Repeat, using the remaining short and long strips, so that you have a total of three red strips, each 51 x 10 inches.

2. To vary the regularity of strips in the ruffle, we made the blue strips of different lengths. Cut two blue strips, each 45 x 10 inches. Cut two additional blue strips, each 44 x 10 inches, and piece them together to form one continuous strip, 88 x 10 inches.

3. Now piece all of the strips together, alternating red with blue, to form one outrageously long strip 10 inches wide. Press all of the seams open. Turn the seam allowances to the wrong side on each 10-inch end, and press.

4. Fold the strip in half lengthwise, wrong sides together, and press. Pin the two raw edges together along the entire length. Run a line of basting stitches ¼ inch from the edges, and another just inside the seam allowance. Pull the threads to form even gathers until the strip measures 4¼ yards long.

5. Pin the gathered strip to the right side of the patchwork quilt top as shown in **Figure H**, beginning and ending at a lower corner. The raw edges of the gathered strip and the patchwork border strips should be even. The folded edge of the gathered strip should extend in toward the center of the patchwork top. Allow plenty of ruffle fabric as you pin around each corner, so the ruffle won't be stretched flat when it is turned outward. Baste the ruffle in place just inside the seam allowance, and whipstitch the folded ends of the ruffle together.

Assembling the quilt

1. Center the piece of quilt batting over the right side of the patchwork top and ruffle assembly. Pin them together, starting at the center and working toward the edges so that everything is smooth and even. The ruffle will be sandwiched between. Baste the batting in place, along the ruffle basting, and remove the pins.

2. Center the flannel backing piece over the batting, and repeat the procedures in step 1 to pin, smooth, and baste the backing to the quilt assembly around the edges.

3. Stitch around all four edges through all thicknesses (patchwork top, ruffle, batting, and backing), leaving a 6-inch opening along the bottom edge (**Figure I**). Turn the quilt right side out, and whipstitch the opening edges together.

4. We tied the quilt at the corners of the squares. Cut sixteen lengths of white yarn, each 12 inches long. Thread the embroidery needle with one of the yarn lengths, and take a stitch through the quilt at the corner of one square, to the back of the quilt. Now return to the front, taking another stitch right next to the previous one. Pull the thread through so that you have two even ends (**Figure J**). Tie the ends in a bow, and knot the loops of the bow so it won't come undone. Repeat at each corner of each square.

Toddler's Chair

A heart-shaped piece is cut from the back of this small wooden chair, then padded and covered with a cross-stitched design, and reinserted into the back. It's a lovely gift that will harmonize with almost any decor.

Materials

10-inch square of ivory-colored 11-count aida cloth.
8-inch square of quilt batting.
Embroidery floss in lime-green, deep pink, and pale pink.
Tapestry needle and scissors.

Figure A

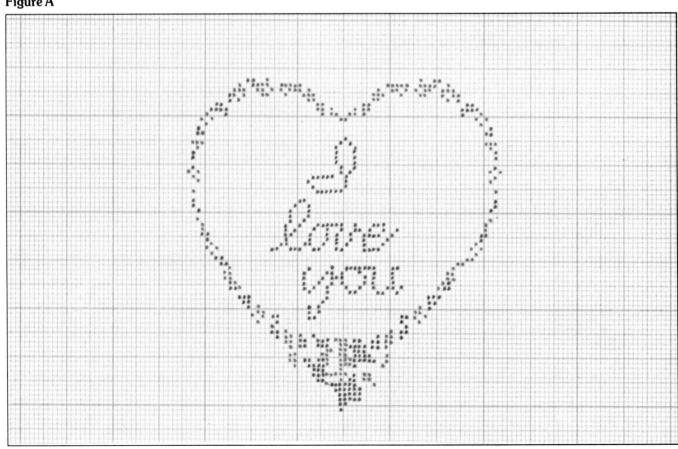

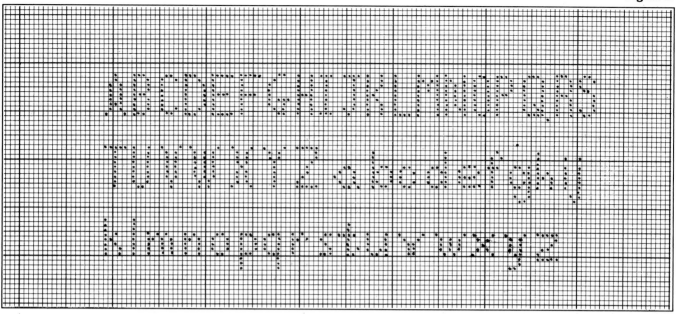

1 square = 1 inch   **Figure C**

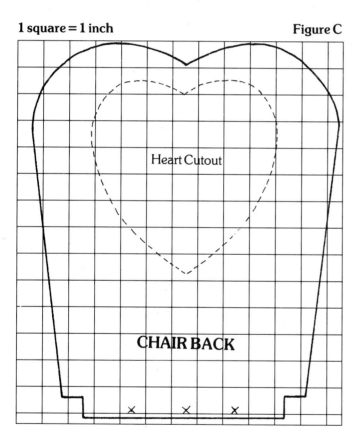

Heart Cutout

CHAIR BACK

Optional materials

You can either make or purchase a chair, or make part and buy part! (How's that for options?) Since we made this one, we can't tell you how much luck you'll have finding one in this style but as long as you find a chair you like, the style really doesn't matter. Just be sure it has a wooden back.

Even without much woodworking experience, you can make this chair – the design is relatively simple. All of the parts can be cut using a saber saw. The only tricky part is cutting the compound miters on the legs, and you can get around that quite easily by purchasing legs that have already been mitered.

To make this chair, you'll need the following:
38-inch length of standard 1 x 12-inch pine.
4-foot length of standard 2 x 2-inch pine.
8-inch square of ¼-inch interior grade plywood.
10-inch length of 1-inch-diameter wooden dowel rod.
Saber saw; phillips screw driver; medium and fine sandpaper; carpenter's wood glue; miter gauge; five No. 6 gauge flathead phillips wood screws, each 1½ inches long; pattern paper; carpenter's rule; wood filler; stain; a can of spray-on sanding sealer; a router with a straight bit; and an electric or hand drill with bits of the following diameters: 1 inch, a bit slightly smaller than the diameter of the screw shanks, and a bit slightly larger than the diameter of the screw heads.

Cross-stitch

1. You'll find a color-coded cross-stitch graph for the heart-shaped border design in **Figure A**. Stitch the design in the center of the aida cloth.

2. Upper and lower case alphabet graphs are provided in **Figure B**. Stitch the child's name on the aida cloth, in the center of the border design. We used green floss for the name. You may prefer to substitute a motto or short poem for the name, but be sure it will fit inside the border before you start to stitch.

Making the chair

Note: If you have purchased a chair, follow only the directions in steps 3, 4, and 11 in this section, and then skip down to "Covering the cutout."

Kids' Stuff   **35**

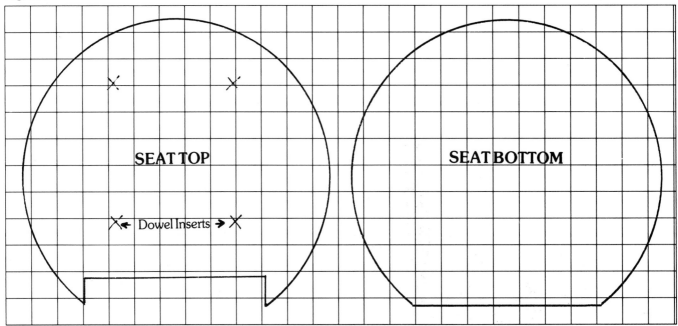

Figure E

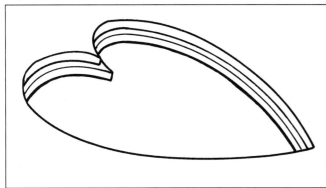

Figure F

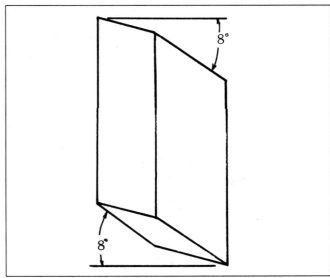

1. A scale drawing for the chair back is given in **Figure C**. Drawings for the upper and lower seat pieces are given in **Figure D**. Enlarge the drawings to full-size paper patterns and transfer the placement markings to the upper seat and chair back patterns.

2. Cut one of each piece from the pine 1 x 12. Transfer the outline of the heart to the wooden chair back, and the placement markings for the 1-inch-diameter holes to the upper seat piece. Glue the two seat pieces together, and clamp them until they dry. Drill a 1-inch-diameter hole through the glued assembly at each placement mark.

3. Cut the heart-shaped opening in the chair back where indicated. To accomplish this, and leave both the cutout piece and chair back in good shape, drill a small hole about 1 inch inside the outline at the upper point of the heart. Insert the saw blade through the hole and cut up to the point. Then cut around the outline, first in one direction and then in the other, so that the cuts meet at the lower point. Save the cutout for later use.

4. The rear edge of the heart-shaped hole is routed to accommodate a plywood cover. Rout all the way around the edge to form a ¼-inch lip (**Figure E**). Use this routed rear edge as a pattern to cut a heart from plywood. Sand, stain, and spray-seal the plywood heart. You now have two wooden heart-shaped pieces; a solid-wood heart and a plywood heart.

5. Cut four legs from the pine 2 x 2, each 10½ inches long. Cut a compound 8 degree miter (don't panic – read on) on both ends of each leg. To do this, simply mark the angle and cut across the end from one corner to the opposite corner (**Figure F**), instead of cutting from side to side as you would for a normal miter. Both ends of each leg should be cut so that they slope in the same direction, as shown.

Figure I

6. Glue the chair back and seats together, fitting the notched lower end of the back into the cutout portion of the upper seat piece (**Figure G**). Allow the assembly to dry slightly, then insert three screws through the lower back, into the upper seat. Insert two screws through the lower seat, up into the chair back. Pre-drill the screw holes to avoid splitting the wood, and pre-drill a shallow socket to accommodate the head of each screw. When the screws have been inserted and countersunk, fill the sockets with wood filler.

7. Cut the 1-inch-diameter dowel rod into four pieces, each 2½ inches long. These will be used to connect the chair seat and legs. To accommodate the dowels, drill a 1-inch-diameter socket, 1 inch deep, straight down into the upper end of each leg as shown in **Figure H**. Because the legs are mitered to stand at an angle, be careful that you do not drill too close to the inside edges, and break through a side of the leg. Glue a dowel pin into each leg.

8. Place the legs under the seat assembly, glueing the dowels into the holes in the seat. The front legs should slant forward and to the sides. The back legs should slant backward and to the sides. Trim the tops of the dowels level with the seat and wipe away any excess glue.

9. Sand the assembled chair thoroughly and carefully. Since pine will often take stain in an uneven way, we sprayed the chair with a light coat of sanding sealer before staining.

10. Sand the heart-shaped solid-wood cutout, giving it a little extra elbow grease around the edges so that it will fit back into the opening when the fabric covering has been added. Spray the cutout with sanding sealer.

Covering the cutout

1. Cut a heart-shaped piece of quilt batting, using the solid-wood cutout as a pattern. Glue the batting to the front of the wooden piece.

2. Center the cross-stitched cloth over the batting and cutout. Hold this assembly together as you pick it up and insert it into the heart-shaped hole in the chair back. (Insert it from the back of the hole toward the front.) If you are satisfied with the placement of the fabric, and everything looks right, carefully remove the cutout from the chair and glue the fabric to the edge in several places. Trim away any fabric that extends past the rear edge of the heart (**Figure I**).

3. Now reinsert the covered cutout, and continue to push it forward until the back of the wooden heart is even with the inner routed edge of the hole.

4. Glue the plywood heart into the back of the opening.

Baby's Birth Record

Delight the proud new parents with this keepsake birth record that can be hung on a wall or displayed on a table. It includes a cross-stitched record of the baby's name, birth date, and weight, and has a framed opening for a photograph.

Materials

¾ yard of yellow gingham with very tiny squares.
1½ yards of 1-inch-wide white eyelet trim.
1 yard of ⅛-inch-wide pink satin ribbon.
8 x 16-inch piece of quilt batting.
Small quantity of polyester fiberfill.
14-count aida cloth in the following amounts and colors:
    4 x 5½-inch piece in white; 3 x 5-inch piece in green;
    5 x 5-inch piece in yellow; 3 x 3-inch piece in baby blue;
    5 x 6-inch piece in brown.
Embroidery floss in blue, white, fuchsia, pink, yellow, and
    light brown.
8 x 16-inch piece of cardboard.
One picture hook and/or a 7 x 9-inch piece of cardboard (to
    hang the birth record or support it on a flat surface).
Tapestry and regular needles, pins, scissors, iron, sewing
    machine, pattern paper, white glue.

Figure A

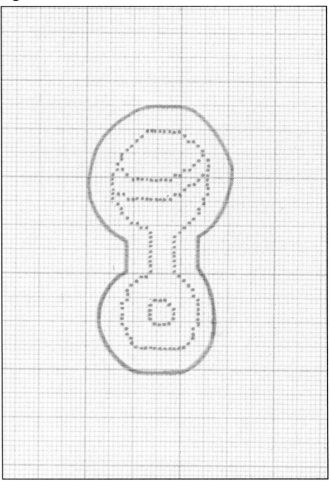

Cross-stitch

1. You'll find cross-stitch graphs for the bear, block, duck, and rattle in **Figure A**. Use white floss to stitch the bear in the center of the brown aida cloth; yellow floss to stitch the block on the blue cloth; light brown floss to stitch the duck on the yellow cloth; and pink floss to stitch the rattle on the green cloth.

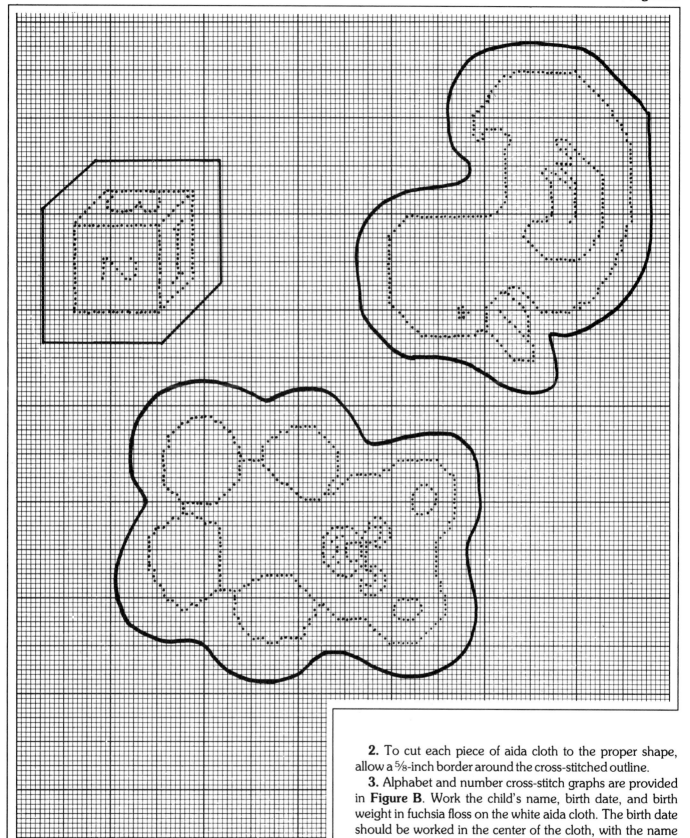

2. To cut each piece of aida cloth to the proper shape, allow a ⅝-inch border around the cross-stitched outline.

3. Alphabet and number cross-stitch graphs are provided in **Figure B**. Work the child's name, birth date, and birth weight in fuchsia floss on the white aida cloth. The birth date should be worked in the center of the cloth, with the name above and the weight below. Leave three blank rows of thread between each line of stitching.

Figure B

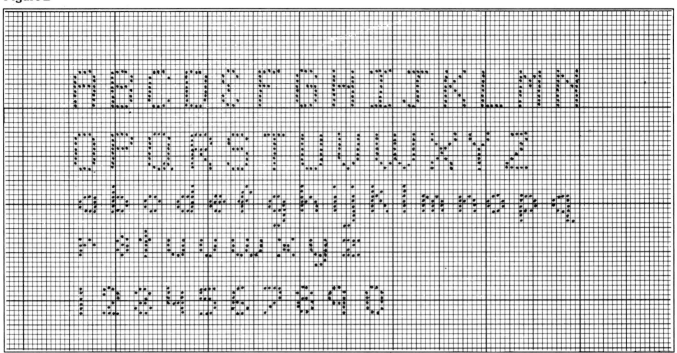

Assembling the ornaments

1. Use the full-size patterns for the bear, block, duck, and rattle to cut a gingham backing piece for each. Cut a 4 x 5½-inch gingham backing piece for the white aida cloth.

2. Place the cross-stitched white aida cloth right side up on a flat surface. Cut an 18-inch length of white eyelet and pin it around the edges of the aida cloth, beginning and ending at a lower corner (**Figure C**). Place the bound edge of the eyelet ¼ inch from the raw edges of the aida cloth, with the scalloped edge pointing inward toward the center. Allow a generous amount of eyelet at each corner, so it won't be stretched flat when it is turned outward. Baste the eyelet in place along the seam lines.

3. Pin the gingham backing right side down over the aida cloth (the eyelet will be sandwiched between), and stitch the seams along all edges, leaving a 2-inch opening along the lower edge (**Figure D**). Clip the corners, turn the assembly right side out, and press gently. Stuff lightly with fiberfill and whipstitch the opening edges together.

4. Follow the procedures described in step 3 to assemble each of the remaining ornaments, omitting the eyelet. Tie a pink ribbon bow around the bear's neck, and another around the rattle. Tie a small bow and tack it to the lower corner of the aida cloth birth record, over the ends of the eyelet.

5. We made a bonnet for the duck from a 9-inch length of eyelet. First, run a line of basting stitches along the bound edge. Fold the eyelet in half widthwise, right sides together, and stitch a narrow seam across the short ends. Turn the eyelet right side out, pull up the basting stitches to form tight gathers, and secure the threads. Tack the bonnet to the top of the duck's head. Tie a small pink ribbon bow and tack it to the top of the bonnet.

Figure C

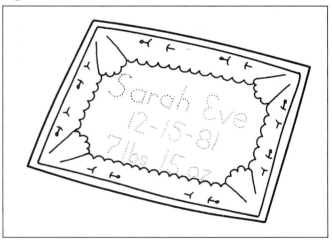

Figure D

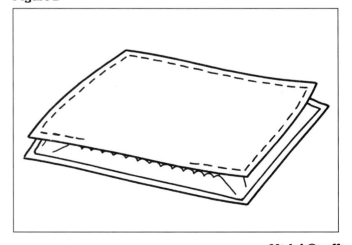

Kids' Stuff

1 square = 1 inch

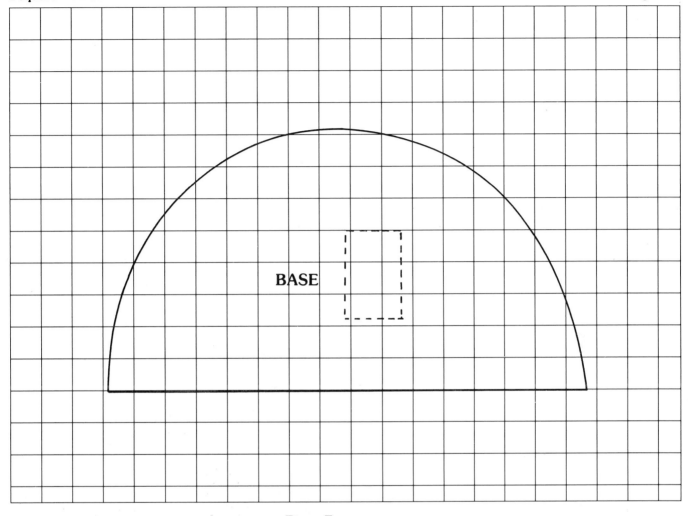

BASE

Making the base

1. A scale drawing for the base pattern is provided in **Figure E**. Enlarge the drawing to a full-size paper pattern, and transfer the dotted window placement lines to the pattern.

2. Use this pattern to cut three pieces from yellow gingham. One of these pieces will be the cover, one the lining, and one the back. Transfer the window placement lines to the wrong side of the cover.

3. Cross-stitch a frame around the window placement lines, on the right side of the cover (**Figure F**). We worked the frame in blue floss, placing the cross-stitches in the tiny gingham squares. Work an inner line of stitches approximately ³⁄₈ inch (six gingham squares) from the placement lines, placing a stitch in every second square. Work an outer line of stitches one square from the inner line, placing a stitch in every square.

4. Pin the cover and lining right sides together, and double stitch along the window placement lines through both layers, using a very small machine stitch.

Kids' Stuff

Figure G

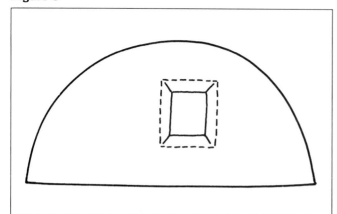

Figure H

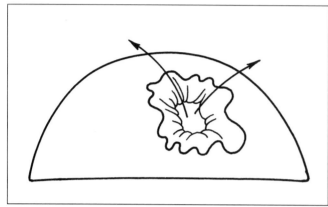

Figure I   1 square = 1 inch

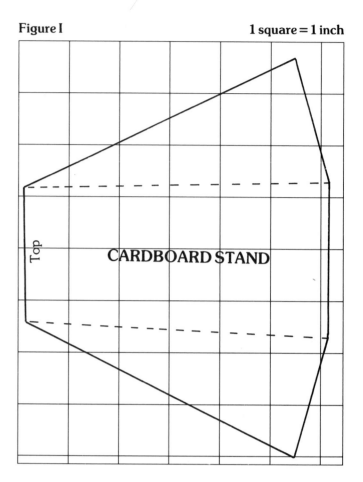

Top

CARDBOARD STAND

5. Cut away both layers of fabric ¼ inch inside the stitching lines (**Figure G**). Clip the corners as close to the stitching as possible without cutting the stitching itself.

6. To turn this assembly right side out, simply stuff one fabric layer through the window opening and pull it through to the opposite side (**Figure H**). Press.

7. Cut a piece of quilt batting ½ inch smaller on all edges than the cover assembly, with a corresponding window opening. To place the batting between the two layers of the cover assembly, stuff one fabric layer through the window in the batting and pull it through until the batting lies between the fabric layers. Smooth the layers flat and pin the cover and lining together around all edges. Baste along the seam line.

8. Pin the gingham back and the cover assembly right sides together and stitch the upper curved seam. Clip the curve in several places, and turn the pieces right sides out. Press the seam allowances to the inside on the straight lower edges.

9. Use this assembly as a pattern to cut a piece of cardboard (but don't cut a window in the cardboard). Insert the cardboard between the gingham back and lining pieces, and mark the position of the window opening on the cardboard. Remove the cardboard, glue a photograph of the baby inside the window placement markings, and replace the cardboard between the gingham layers. Whipstitch the lower edges together.

Finishing touches

1. Cut a 26-inch length of eyelet trim and whipstitch it along the curved edge, on the front of the birth record. Turn the raw ends to the back.

2. Tack the stuffed ornaments to the front, following the arrangement pictured here or another one that pleases you.

3. Cut four 6-inch lengths of blue embroidery floss. Tie each in a bow and tack the bows at the corners of the window opening, inside the cross-stitched frame.

4. Attach a picture hanger or cardboard stand (or both) to the back of the birth record. A scale drawing of the stand pattern is given in **Figure I**. Enlarge the drawing to a full-size paper pattern.

5. Cut one stand from cardboard. Use the same pattern to cut two pieces from gingham, each ½ inch larger on all edges than the pattern. Place the gingham pieces right sides together and stitch the seams along the two long side edges and the top edge. Clip the corners and turn the pieces right sides out. Press the remaining seam allowances to the inside.

6. Insert the cardboard stand between the gingham pieces and whipstitch the opening edges together. Fold the wings along the dotted lines, both in the same direction. Glue the center portion of the stand to the back of the birth record, and secure it with clothespins or clamps while it dries.

42

Kids' Stuff

Tooth Fairy Pillow

This little character will hold lost teeth in safekeeping for the Tooth Fairy, and will also help remind a child to brush regularly. The pillow is 10 inches tall, with a cross-stitched face and tooth pocket, and is a good project for beginners.

Materials

½ yard of pink cotton print fabric.
7 x 6-inch piece of white 11-count aida cloth.
5 x 4-inch piece of white 14- or 18-count aida cloth.
½ yard of ⅜-inch-wide pink satin ribbon.
7-inch length of ¾-inch-wide white eyelet trim.
1-inch length of ½-inch-wide elastic.
Embroidery floss in red, pink, light blue, dark blue, and black.
Small skein of pink yarn.
Small quantity of polyester fiberfill.
Child's toothbrush.
Small tube of toothpaste.
White thread, tapestry and regular needles, embroidery hoop, sewing machine, pins, iron, scissors, and pattern paper.

Cross-stitch

You'll find a color-coded cross-stitch graph for the facial features in **Figure A**. Stitch the features in the center of the 11-count aida cloth.

The tooth pocket will be cut from the smaller piece of aida cloth. Work from the alphabet graph provided in **Figure B** to cross-stitch a child's name on this piece. You may prefer to stitch a message, such as "MY TOOTH," but it will have to be a short one since the cloth will later be cut to the size of the pocket pattern (shown full size in **Figure C**).

Figure A

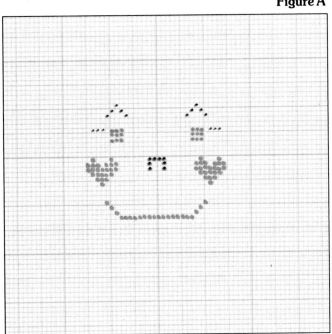

Figure B

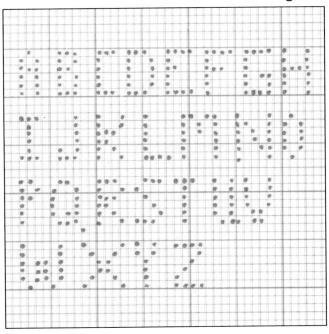

Figure C

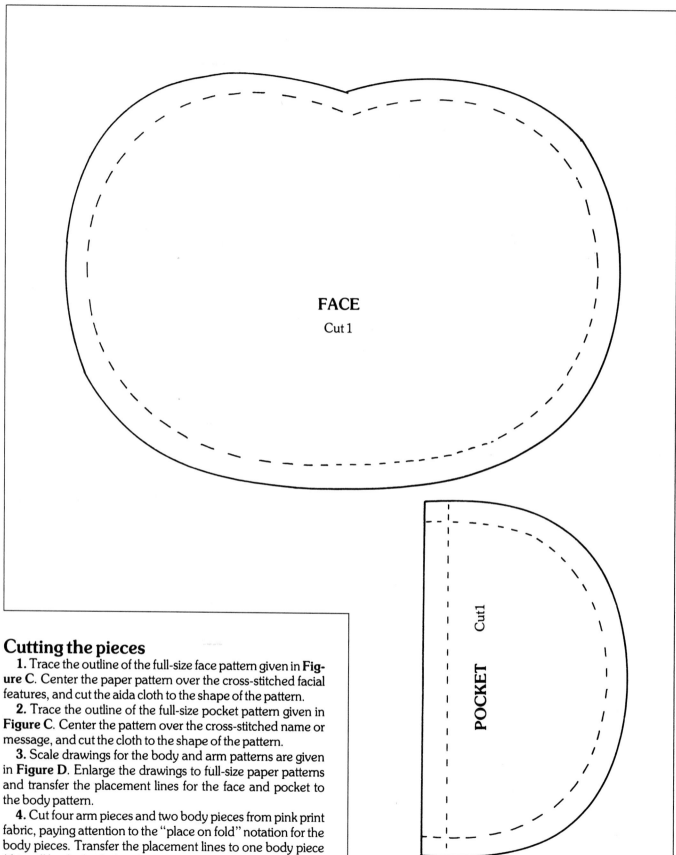

FACE

Cut 1

POCKET Cut1

Cutting the pieces

1. Trace the outline of the full-size face pattern given in **Figure C**. Center the paper pattern over the cross-stitched facial features, and cut the aida cloth to the shape of the pattern.

2. Trace the outline of the full-size pocket pattern given in **Figure C**. Center the pattern over the cross-stitched name or message, and cut the cloth to the shape of the pattern.

3. Scale drawings for the body and arm patterns are given in **Figure D**. Enlarge the drawings to full-size paper patterns and transfer the placement lines for the face and pocket to the body pattern.

4. Cut four arm pieces and two body pieces from pink print fabric, paying attention to the "place on fold" notation for the body pieces. Transfer the placement lines to one body piece (this will be the body front).

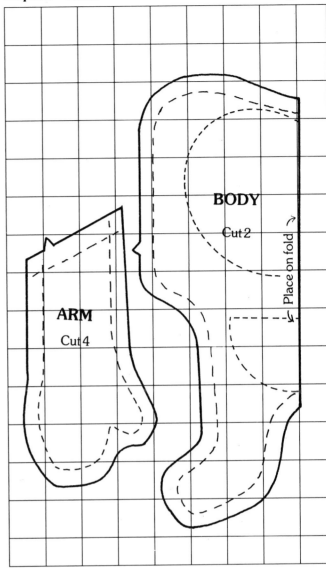

BODY

Cut 2

Place on fold

ARM

Cut 4

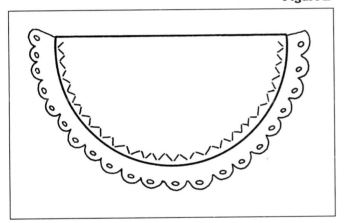

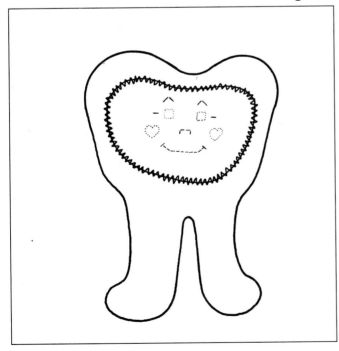

Making the body front

Note: All seam allowances are ½ inch unless otherwise specified in the instructions.

1. Begin by preparing the cross-stitched aida cloth pieces. For the face, simply staystitch close to the raw edge. For the pocket, turn ¼-inch seam allowances to the wrong side on both the straight and curved edges, and press. Place the bound edge of the eyelet trim under the pocket along the lower curved edge (**Figure E**) and baste in place. Stitch the eyelet to the pocket using widely-spaced zigzag stitches.

2. Place the body front right side up on a flat surface. Pin and then baste the cross-stitched face to the body, right side up inside the placement lines (**Figure F**). Stitch the face to the body, using closely-spaced zigzag stitches lapped over the raw edge of the aida cloth.

3. Pin the pocket right side up over the body, inside the pocket placement lines. Topstitch close to the lower curved edge, using a small straight stitch.

Figure G

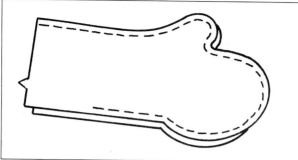

Figure H

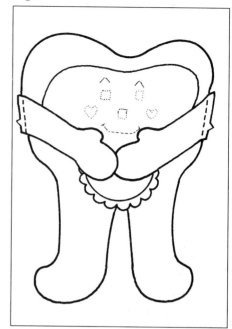

Figure I

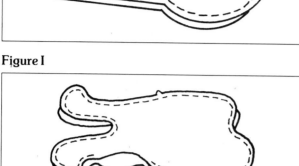

Figure J

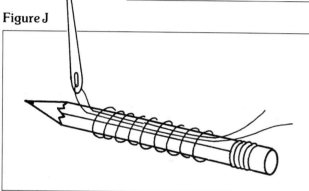

Figure K

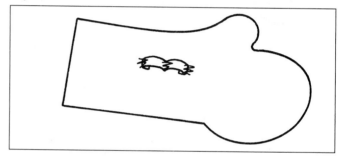

Assembling the body

1. Place the two arm pieces right sides together and stitch the seam around the long contoured edge (**Figure G**). Leave a 2-inch portion unstitched on one side, and leave the straight shoulder edge open and unstitched as shown. Clip the curves and turn the stitched arm right side out. Repeat these procedures using the remaining two arm pieces.

2. Pin the two stitched arms to the right side of the front body (thumbs up), matching notches (**Figure H**). Baste just inside the seam allowance.

3. Pin the remaining body piece over the front body and arms, placing right sides together and matching notches. The arms will be sandwiched between the body pieces. Stitch all the way around the outer edge, leaving a 3-inch opening on the outside of one leg (**Figure I**). Be careful not to catch the eyelet pocket trim in the seam.

4. Turn the stitched body right side out through the opening. Stuff the body and arms tightly with fiberfill. (Stuff the body through the opening in the leg, and each arm through the opening near the shoulder.) Whipstitch the edges of each opening together.

Finishing details

1. This tooth fairy pillow has curly pink hair. To create the hair, you'll be working with a needle and thread, and a continuous length of pink yarn. Begin by stitching the end of the yarn to the edge of the aida cloth, at eye level.

2. Wrap the yarn ten or twelve times around a fat pencil or other round object. Insert the needle between the loops of yarn and the pencil, and pull it out through the opposite end (**Figure J**). Remove the pencil and take another stitch into the head to secure the curl. Continue making curls in this manner all the way along the upper edge of the face, until you reach eye level on the opposite side.

3. Tie the pink ribbon in a bow and tack it to one side of the head, just above the hairline.

4. The elastic is attached to one arm as a toothbrush holder. Pin the elastic to the inside of one arm, just above the wrist. Stitch it in place across the ends and center (**Figure K**), so that it will hold two brushes.

5. Bend the arms forward and tack them to the body. Insert the toothbrush handle through one of the loops formed by the elastic. Insert the toothpaste tube between the body and the opposite arm.

Kids' Stuff

Friendship Pillow

Tell someone how much you care! This frilly pillow carries a cross-stitched message of friendship — and if the frills don't go with your friend's decor, just sew up the pillow without them.

Materials

½ yard of navy blue pin-dot cotton fabric.
1¾ yards of 3-inch-wide white eyelet trim.
11 x 9-inch piece of ivory-colored 14-count aida cloth.
11 x 9-inch piece of white cotton broadcloth.
16-ounce bag of polyester fiberfill.
Pink and navy blue cotton embroidery floss.
White sewing thread, tapestry needle, embroidery hoop, sewing machine, pins, scissors, and measuring tape.

Cross-stitch

Cross-stitch the verse and border design on the aida cloth, following the stitching graph provided in **Figure A**. We worked the border hearts in pink floss, and all other stitches in blue.

Figure A

Figure B

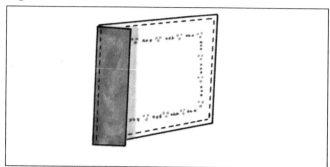

Sewing the pillow

Note: All seam allowances are ½ inch.

The pillow front consists of a center panel (the cross-stitched aida cloth), lined with broadcloth and bordered on all four edges with pin-dot fabric.

1. Cut two borders, each 9 x 3 ½ inches; and two borders, each 16 x 3½ inches.

2. Place the cross-stitched aida cloth right side up over the white broadcloth lining and baste the two pieces together ¼ inch from the raw edges.

3. Pin one short border to one side edge of the aida cloth, placing right sides together and raw edges even as shown in **Figure B**. Stitch the seam. Press the border open and press the seam allowances toward the center panel. Repeat this step to attach the remaining short border to the opposite side.

4. Follow the same procedures to attach the longer borders to the upper and lower edges of the aida cloth and short borders, as shown in **Figure C**. Press the borders open, and press the seam allowances toward the center panel.

5. Pin the bound edge of the eyelet trim along the raw edges of the assembled pillow front **(Figure D)**, placing right sides together and beginning and ending at the center of the bottom edge. (The scalloped edge of the eyelet should extend in toward the center of the pillow front.) Allow a very generous amount of eyelet at each corner, so that it will lie flat when turned outward. Baste the eyelet in place, and stitch the ends of the eyelet together as shown, where they meet at the center bottom.

6. Cut one pillow back, 14 x 16 inches, from the pin-dot fabric. Pin the back over the assembled front, placing right sides together. The eyelet will be sandwiched between. Stitch the side and top seams, leaving the bottom edge open and unstitched **(Figure E)**.

7. Clip the corners and turn the pillow casing right side out. Press gently with a steam iron. On the remaining raw edges, turn the seam allowances to the wrong side and press. Stuff the pillow casing with fiberfill and whipstitch the turned bottom edges together.

Figure C

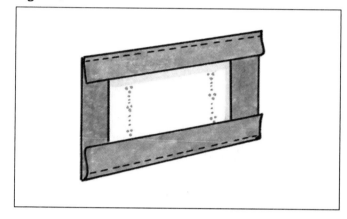

Figure D

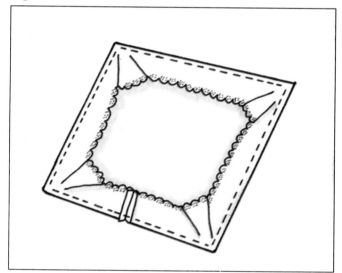

Figure E

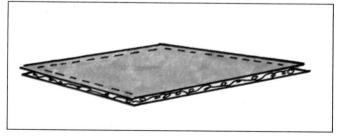

48

Butterfly Bedside Organizer

This handy organizer has pockets galore to hold all that necessary bedtime paraphernalia — glasses, tissues, books, pens, paper, ad infinitum. Just slip the upper flap between your mattress and box spring, and it's all at your fingertips!

Materials

1⅝ yards of 45-inch-wide mustard-colored corduroy.

11 x 22½-inch piece of ivory-colored 14-count aida cloth.

2½ yards of 2-inch-wide pre-gathered ruffling. We used ruffling made from ivory-colored cotton fabric, with deep yellow pin dots.

10 x 21½-inch piece of thin quilt batting.

Embroidery floss in deep yellow, pale yellow, tan, light brown, kelly green, medium green, and pale green.

Tapestry and regular needles, pins, scissors, iron, sewing machine, thread to match the fabrics.

Cross-stitch

A color-coded cross-stitch graph for the butterfly and flower design is provided in **Figure A**. Stitch the design on the aida cloth, centered between all edges. Staystitch ¼ inch from each edge.

Cutting the pieces

All of the pieces for the organizer are simple rectangles. We suggest that you label them as you cut, to prevent confusion when you are assembling them. All pieces are cut from corduroy, and all seam allowances are ½ inch. A cutting diagram is provided in **Figure B**.

1. Cut two backing pieces, each 31 x 22½ inches.
2. Cut two upper pocket pieces, each 5½ x 22½ inches.
3. Cut two middle pocket pieces, each 8½ x 22½ inches.
4. Cut one lower pocket piece, 11 x 22½ inches.

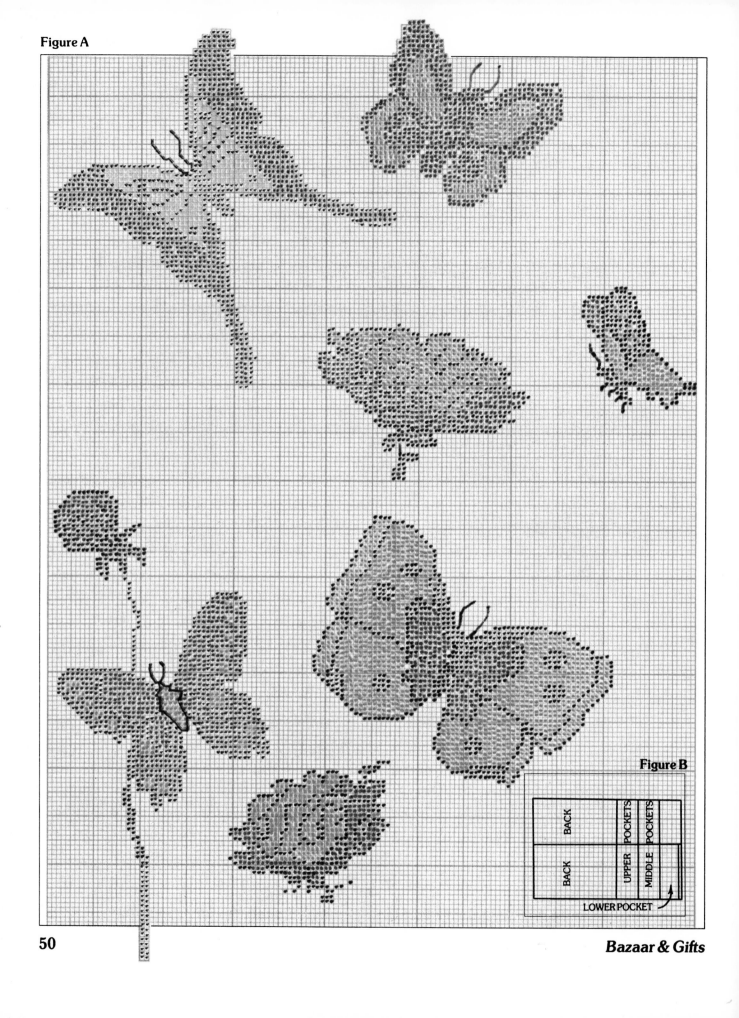

Figure B

	BACK	UPPER	POCKETS	
BACK		POCKETS		
	BACK	UPPER	MIDDLE	POCKETS
LOWER POCKET				

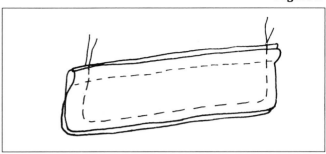

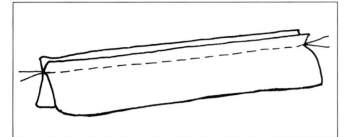

Figure C

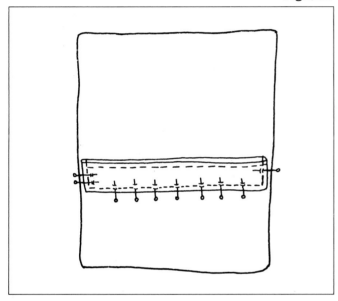

Figure E

Figure F

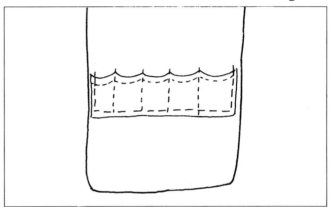

Figure G

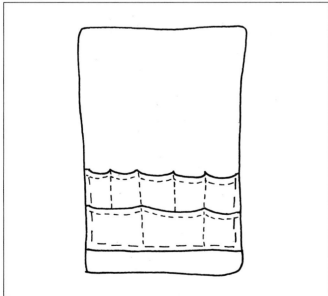

Assembly

This project is quite simple to make. The upper and middle pockets are sewn into the lined backing, and the lower cross-stitched pocket is whipstitched to the assembled organizer.

1. Pin the two upper pocket pieces right sides together and stitch the seam on one long edge only (**Figure C**). Turn the pieces right sides out and press. Pin and then baste them together around the three remaining open edges, and topstitch ³⁄₈ inch from the seamed upper edge (**Figure D**).

2. Follow the same procedures to prepare the middle pocket pieces.

3. Place one backing piece right side up on a flat surface. Pin the upper pocket to the backing piece, placing the topstitched edge of the pocket approximately 16 inches from the lower end (**Figure E**). Baste along the two side seam lines and stitch along the lower seam line.

4. We divided the pocket into five smaller sections by running four evenly-spaced lines of stitching from top to bottom, through the pocket and backing (**Figure F**).

5. The middle pocket is attached in the same manner. Pin it to the backing piece, placing the topstitched edge of the pocket approximately 13½ inches from the lower end of the backing. (It will overlap the upper pocket by several inches.) Baste along the side seam lines and stitch along the lower seam line.

6. We divided the middle pocket into three sections (two large and one small) as shown in **Figure G**. Use the same stitching technique described in step 4, but run only two lines of stitching, aligning them with two of the stitching lines on the upper pocket as shown.

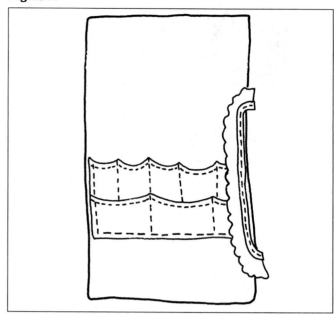

7. Cut two 12-inch lengths of ruffling. Pin one length to the right-hand edge of the backing piece and pockets, placing right sides together, as shown in **Figure H**. Begin at a point approximately 4 inches above the top of the upper pocket, and work downward over both pockets. Place the bound edge of the ruffling even with the raw edge of the backing, so that the ruffled edge extends inward. Curve the ruffling outward at each end as shown, so that when the organizer is stitched and turned the ruffle will have finished ends. Baste along the seam line. Attach the remaining 12-inch length of ruffling to the opposite side in the same manner.

8. Pin the remaining backing piece right side down over this assembly (the pockets and ruffles will be sandwiched between the backing pieces). Stitch the seams on the two long edges and the upper short edge, leaving the lower short edge open and unstitched. Clip the corners, turn the assembly right side out, and press. Press the seam allowances to the inside on the remaining raw edges.

9. To keep the two backing layers from slipping when the organizer is in use, run several rows of stitching across the upper flap portion as shown in **Figure I**.

Adding the lower pocket

1. Press the seam allowances to the wrong side on all four edges of the cross-stitched aida cloth. Pin the bound edge of the ruffling to the right side of the aida cloth (**Figure J**), so that the ruffle extends out beyond the turned edges of the cloth. Begin and end at a lower corner, turning a hem allowance to the wrong side at each end of the ruffling. Stitch along each edge of the ruffle binding, and whipstitch the turned ends together.

2. Press the seam allowances to the wrong side on all four edges of the corduroy lower pocket piece. Pin the corduroy and aida cloth pieces wrong sides together, sandwiching the quilt batting between them. Whipstitch the upper edges together, and leave the remaining edges pinned.

3. Place the lower pocket over the organizer, with lower and side edges even. The lower pocket will overlap the middle pocket by several inches. Pin them together along the side and lower edges by removing and replacing the pins already holding the edges of the pocket. Whipstitch the side and lower edges of the pocket and organizer together.

4. Cut a 1 x 14-inch piece of corduroy for the bow. Fold it in half lengthwise, placing right sides together. Stitch diagonally across one short end and close to the long edge, leaving the remaining short edge open and unstitched. Turn right side out (use a long thin object to help turn the narrow tube) and press. Tuck the raw edge to the inside on the remaining open end, and whipstitch. Tie the strip in a bow and tack the bow to the top center point of the aida cloth, stitching through all layers of the lower pocket and both corduroy layers of the middle pocket.

Figure I

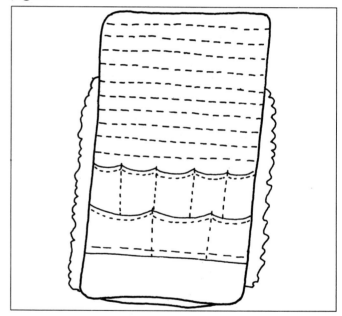

Figure J

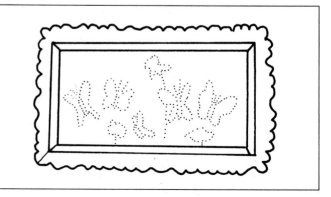

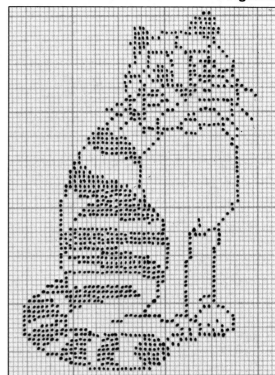

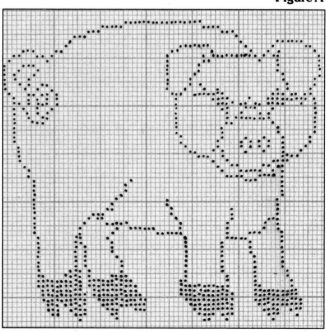

Country Critter Potholders

These charming, oversized, inexpensive potholders are as easy to make as instant mashed potatoes. By varying the colors of the fabric and embroidery floss, you can coordinate the potholders with the color scheme of any kitchen!

Materials

To make all five potholders, you need the following:

¾ yard of 45-inch-wide cotton fabric — we used a brown patchwork calico print.

Five squares of brown 14-count aida cloth, each 9 x 9 inches.

¾ yard of coordinated fabric-covered cording (for the hanging loops).

5 yards of corded piping (to inset between the aida cloth and fabric).

Five squares of quilt batting, each 10 x 10 inches.

Tapestry needle, white embroidery floss, sewing thread to match the fabric, scissors, straight pins, steam iron, and a sewing machine with a zipper foot attachment.

Cross-stitch

You'll find a cross-stitch graph for the five potholder designs (hen, rooster, cow, cat, and pig) in **Figure A**. Work each of the designs on a separate 9-inch square of aida cloth. We cross-stitched all of the animals using white floss only, so no colors are indicated on the graph.

Figure A

Figure A

Figure A

Sewing the potholders

1. The cross-stitched center front of each potholder is bordered by four strips of fabric. Cut two strips for the top and bottom, each 9 inches long and 3½ inches wide. Cut two strips for the sides, each 14 inches long and 3½ inches wide.

2. Pin a length of corded piping around the aida cloth center, ½ inch from the edges. The raw edges of the piping should be placed toward the edges. Begin and end the piping at a corner, overlapping the ends (**Figure B**).

3. Place the aida cloth center with pinned piping face up, and pin one short border strip face down over the top edge. The piping will be sandwiched between the two layers. Stitch a ½-inch seam as shown in **Figure C**. Use a zipper foot on your machine, and stitch as close as possible to the cord inside the piping.

4. Repeat the procedure to attach the remaining 9-inch strip to the bottom. Turn the border strips outward and press the seams open.

5. Pin one 14-inch strip over one side edge of the aida cloth and shorter strips, placing right sides together. Stitch, turn the strip outward, and press the seam open. Repeat the procedure to attach the remaining strip to the opposite side.

6. Repeat steps 1 through 5 to complete the front for each of the remaining four potholders.

Figure C

Figure D

Finishing

1. Cut a 5-inch length of fabric-covered cording for the hanging loop. Fold the cording in half and baste it to the upper left corner of the potholder front, overlapping the ends at the seam allowance as shown in **Figure D**.

2. Cut an 11-inch-square fabric back. Place the back and potholder front (with attached hanging loop) right sides together. Stitch a ½-inch seam across the sides and top, leaving the bottom edge open and unstitched. Clip the corners, turn the potholder right side out, and press. Turn the remaining raw edges to the inside along the seam allowance and press.

3. Insert the 10-inch square of batting inside the potholder through the opening at the bottom. Topstitch ¼ inch from the outer edges on all four sides.

4. Repeat steps 1 through 3 to assemble the remaining four potholders.

Padded
Picture Frame

Here's a very special frame to cross-stitch for your child's sports photos. It is made to resemble a soccer ball, and will fit right in among the trophies and ribbons in his or her room.

Materials

Four pieces of medium-weight cardboard, each at least 8 inches square.

One piece of 14-count ivory-colored aida cloth, 10 inches square.

½ yard of muslin fabric.

2 yards of single-fold woven black nylon braid, ½ inch wide.

One piece of bonded quilt batting, 10 inches square.

Glue gun and hot-melt adhesive. You can substitute white glue, but you will need clamps or clothespins to secure your work until the glue dries.

Black embroidery floss.

Tapestry and sewing needles, black and ivory thread, scissors, ruler, iron, and pins.

Cross-stitch

1. A graph for the soccer ball cross-stitch design is given in **Figure A**. The center of the design will measure 2⅜ x 4½ inches when complete. Check the dimensions of the picture you intend to frame, and adjust the graph if necessary.

2. Cross-stitch the design in the center of the ivory aida cloth using a tapestry needle and black embroidery floss. Gently press the finished cross-stitch on the wrong side using a steam setting.

Figure A

Centerline

56

Bazaar & Gifts

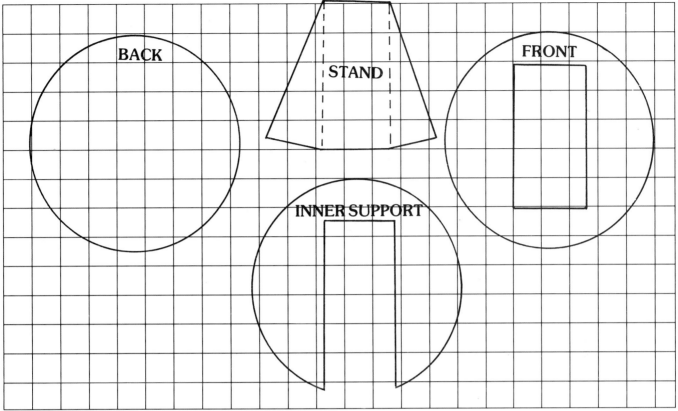

Making the frame

1. Enlarge the scale drawings given in **Figure B** to full size and cut one of each piece from cardboard.

2. Use the cardboard back piece as a pattern to cut two muslin circles, adding a 2-inch border around the circumference. The border will provide enough extra fabric to overlap the edges of the frame.

3. Center the cross-stitched aida cloth over one muslin circle, placing right sides together. Sew the two pieces together, stitching just inside the cross-stitched center rectangle (**Figure C**), using a very small machine stitch.

4. To "open" the window, cut away both layers of fabric inside the stitched rectangle, ¼ inch inside the stitching line. Clip the corners as close to the stitching as possible without cutting the stitching itself.

5. To turn this assembly right sides out, simply stuff the muslin circle through the window opening and pull it out on the opposite side (**Figure D**). Press the two layers. Trim the aida cloth to the size of the muslin circle.

6. Cut a piece of quilt batting the same size as the cardboard front, with a corresponding center hole. Place the aida cloth assembly right side up on a flat surface and stack the cardboard and batting on top. Hold the cardboard and batting together and pull the aida cloth layer through the center opening. The batting will now be between the aida and cardboard layers, and the muslin will be under the cardboard. Smooth the layers flat, pin the aida and muslin together, and baste around the circumference, enclosing the batting and cardboard.

Figure C

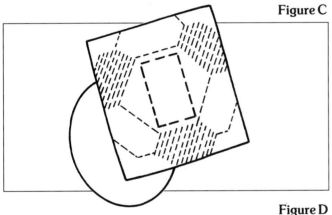

Figure D

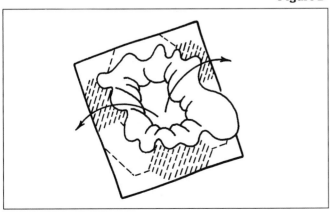

Figure E

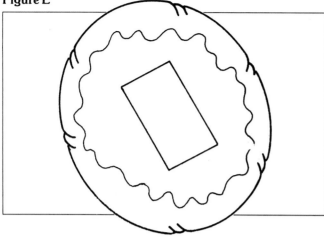

7. Pull the fabric edges to the back and glue them to the muslin fabric, stretching and smoothing the cross-stitched front as you work. Glue the fabric at the top and bottom first, and then at the two sides. Check the front side of the assembly occasionaly to make sure you have not pulled the design off center, and continue to glue at opposite points on the circle, between the previously attached points (**Figure E**). If you are using white glue, it will be necessary to clamp the glued fabric with clothespins or straight pins until the glue has dried.

8. Glue the cardboard inner support piece to the wrong side of the assembled frame front, making sure the opening for the picture is at the center bottom of the frame as shown in **Figure F**.

9. To make a finished back for the frame, place the cardboard back piece in the center of the remaining muslin circle. Pull the fabric edges upward and glue them to the cardboard, stretching and smoothing the fabric as you work. Again, clamp the glued fabric until it dries if you are using white glue.

Finishing

1. Use the cardboard stand to cut two pieces from muslin, each ½ inch larger on all edges than the stand. Place the muslin pieces together and stitch ½-inch seams along the two long sides and the top edge. Clip the corners and turn the pieces right sides out. Press ½-inch seam allowances to the inside along the remaining raw edges.

2. Insert the cardboard stand between the muslin pieces and whipstitch the opening edges together. Fold the wings along the dotted lines, both in the same direction. Glue the center portion of the stand to the muslin-covered side of the frame back assembly, and secure it with clothespins or clamps while it dries.

3. Encase the outer edges of the completed frame front and frame back assemblies in black nylon braid, beginning and ending at the center bottom. Glue the braid in place.

4. Glue the completed frame front and back assemblies wrong sides together, clamping them until they are dry. To give a finished look to the frame, whipstitch the outer folded edges of the black braid together using small invisible stitches (**Figure G**), leaving an opening at the bottom so that you can insert the photo.

Figure F

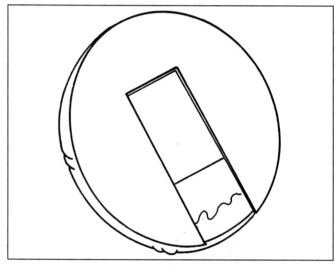

Figure G

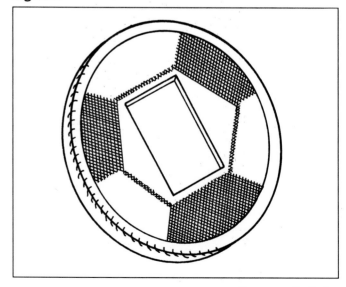

Desk Accessories

Coordinate and organize your desk with these colorful accessories. This is a great way to use up remnants of aida cloth, embroidery floss, and fabric.

Materials

To make the accessories shown here, you'll need three cardboard boxes; one for pencils, one for note paper, and one to hold a small clock. Exact sizes are not crucial, as long as each box is an appropriate size for the function it will serve. We have specified the materials you'll need if you wish to reproduce the pieces shown here. If you already have a set of accessories, you may simply wish to make fabric covers and cross-stitched labels. Or, you may wish to purchase a set of plastic accessories and cover them.

Three pieces of ivory-colored 14-count aida cloth; $1\frac{5}{8}$ x 4 inches for the note holder, $3\frac{3}{8}$ x $4\frac{1}{4}$ inches for the pencil holder, and $5\frac{3}{4}$ x $7\frac{1}{4}$ inches for the clock.

Three cardboard boxes with lids; $4\frac{1}{2}$ x $6\frac{1}{4}$ x 1 inch for the note holder, 3 x $3\frac{1}{4}$ x $4\frac{3}{4}$ inches for the pencil holder, and 4 x $5\frac{1}{2}$ x $1\frac{1}{2}$ inches for the clock.

$\frac{3}{4}$ yard of medium-weight fabric to cover the boxes. We used a peach-colored cotton blend with a small floral pattern in green, gold, and rust.

Embroidery floss in three colors to coordinate with the fabric. We used peach, rust, and brown.

$5\frac{3}{4}$ x $7\frac{1}{4}$-inch piece of unbleached muslin.

Small amount of polyester fiberfill.

$\frac{5}{8}$ yard of single-fold, $\frac{1}{2}$-inch-wide ivory-colored braid trim.

A circular battery-operated clock, approximately $1\frac{1}{4}$ inches in diameter.

Tapestry and regular needles, glue gun with hot-melt adhesive (or white glue), sewing machine, scissors, white sewing thread, steam iron.

Figure A

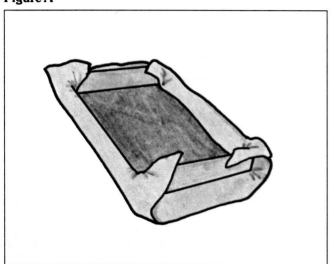

Figure B

Figure C

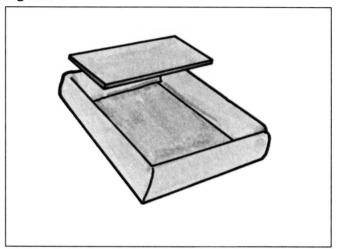

Covering the boxes

To cover each of these boxes with fabric, begin by placing the box on the wrong side of the fabric. Pull the fabric up over the open top edges of the box, and trim it off about 2 inches beyond the top of the box. Glue the fabric to any two opposite sides (**Figure A**), lapping the edges over the top and glueing them to the inside. Now glue the fabric to the remaining two sides, folding it neatly so that the exposed folds follow the straight corner lines (**Figure B**).

At this point the procedure will depend on the depth of the box. For a shallow box, the fabric lapped to the inside will completely cover the inner sides of the box, so you can skip down to the next paragraph. For a deep box, you will need to line the inner sides with a separate piece of fabric. Cut a piece of fabric 2 inches wider than the depth of the box and 2 inches longer than the perimeter. Turn the top 1 inch to the wrong side of the fabric and press. Make 1-inch-deep clips along the bottom edge at ½-inch intervals. Turn a ½-inch allowance to the wrong side of the fabric on each end and press. Glue the fabric inside the box, with top edges even, lapping one end over the other.

To finish, cut a piece from the lid, making it slightly smaller than the bottom of the box. Cut a piece of fabric 1 inch larger on all edges than the cardboard. Glue the cardboard to the center of the wrong side of the fabric, lap the fabric edges to the opposite side, and glue them down. Insert the cardboard into the box, fabric side up, and push it all the way down to the bottom.

Making the note holder

1. Cover the box as described. Cut a piece from the lid to fit across the top as a lip (**Figure C**). Cover the lip with fabric, lapping the raw edges underneath, and glue the covered lip over the top of the box, flush with one short edge.

Figure E

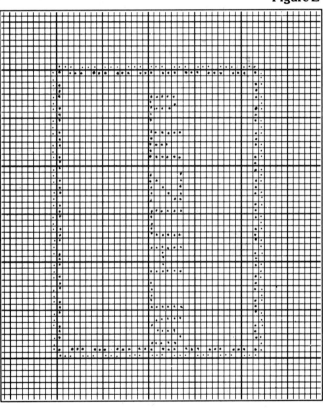

Figure D

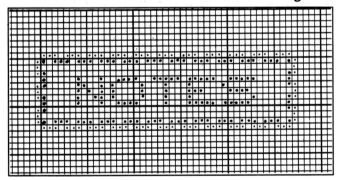

2. A cross-stitch graph for the bordered label is provided in **Figure D**. Stitch the word NOTES in the center of the 4 x 1⅝-inch aida cloth, and then work the border design.

3. Staystitch ¼ inch from each edge of the cloth. Clip the corners and turn the raw edges to the wrong side along the staystitching. Press gently. Topstitch close to each folded edge.

4. Glue the label to the center of the lip.

Making the pencil box

1. Cover the box as described.

2. A cross-stitch graph for the label is provided in **Figure E**. Stitch the word PENCILS vertically in the center of the specified aida cloth, and then work the border design.

3. Staystitch ¼ inch from each edge. Clip the corners and turn the raw edges to the wrong side along the staystitching. Press gently. Topstitch close to each folded edge.

4. Glue the label to one side of the pencil box.

Figure F

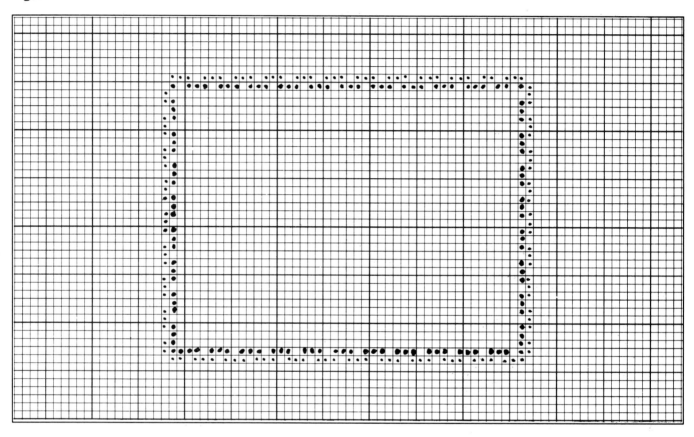

Making the clock case

1. Cover the box as described. There is no need to cut and cover a lining for the bottom of the box. The lid of the box will later be used as a backing for the clock and cross-stitched cover.

2. A stitching graph for the cover is provided in **Figure F**. Center and stitch the border design on the remaining piece of aida cloth.

3. Use the clock face as a pattern to draw a circle in the center of the muslin. Pin the muslin to the right side of the aida cloth.

4. To create a window opening for the clock face, first sew the muslin and aida cloth together, stitching along the circle you have just drawn using a very small machine stitch (**Figure G**).

Figure G

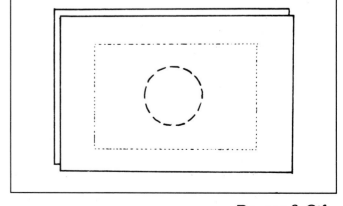

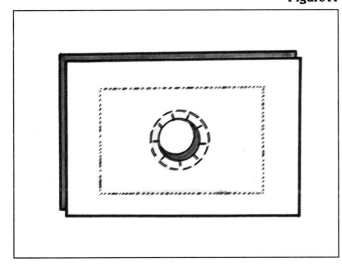

Figure I

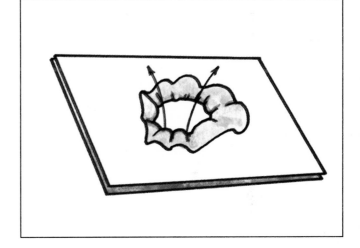

5. To open the window, cut away both layers of fabric inside the stitched circle, ¼ inch from the stitching line. Clip the allowance in several places as close to the stitching as possible without cutting the stitching itself (**Figure H**).

6. To turn the assembly right side out, simply stuff the muslin rectangle through the window opening and pull it out on the opposite side (**Figure I**). Press the seamed circular window opening and baste the two fabric layers together ¼ inch from each raw edge.

7. Use the back of the clock as a pattern to cut a circular opening in the center of the box lid. The hole should allow you access to the back of the clock (to change batteries), but it should not allow the clock to slip through. Trim off the edges of the lid so that it will slide easily inside the fabric-covered box. Insert the back of the clock into the hole.

8. Glue fiberfill to the top of the lid around the clock, to the depth of the clock face. Place the cross-stitched cover (muslin side down) over the fiberfill and clock, so that the clock face shows through the open window. Glue the raw fabric edges to the back of the cardboard, being careful not to pull the window opening off center as you work. Glue braid trim around the edges of the covered lid, overlapping the ends at a bottom corner (**Figure J**).

9. Stuff fiberfill into the fabric-covered clock case to a depth of about 1½ inch. Insert the cover assembly inside the box.

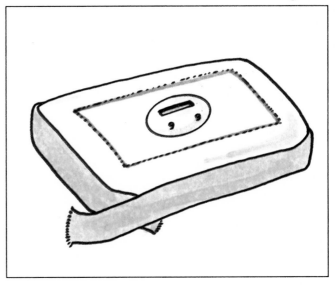

Herb Garden

Homegrown herbs make a delicious difference in what comes out of the kitchen. A fabric-covered miniature window box (with a whimsical cross-stitched label) is the perfect place to grow them!

Materials

One plastic tray or cardboard box, approximately 2 feet long and 4 to 5 inches in height and depth. The plastic trays sold in paint and wallpaper stores for dipping whole rolls of wallpaper are perfect for this, but cardboard will do if you line it with heavy plastic or foil.

⅝ yard of 36-inch-wide brown calico print fabric. You may need more or less if your tray is considerably different in size than specified above.

16 x 3¾-inch piece of ivory-colored 14-count aida cloth.

1 yard of green terrycloth corded piping.

Embroidery floss in burnt orange, medium green, and dark brown.

Five small herb plants, each in a 4 x 4-inch pot with a saucer to catch the water overflow and protect your plants from the glue. Make sure the pots and saucers will fit inside the tray you plan to use.

Glue gun and a small quantity of hot-melt adhesive, or white glue. If you use white glue, you'll need several clothespins to use as temporary clamps.

Tapestry and regular sewing needles, green thread, scissors, pinking shears (optional), pins, sewing machine.

Cross-stitch

A color-coded cross-stitch graph for the words and border design that make up the herb garden label are provided in **Figure A**. Stitch the label in the center of the aida cloth. Staystitch ¼ inch from all edges of the cloth.

Figure A

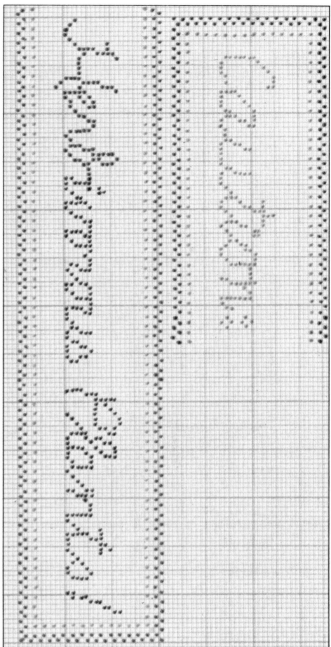

Finishing the label

1. Pin the corded piping on the right side of the fabric around the edge of the aida cloth, beginning and ending at a lower corner (**Figure B**). The raw edges of the piping should be even with the edges of the cloth, except at the corners where you can simply bend the piping around in smooth curves. The corded edge of the piping should extend in toward the center of the cloth, and the ends should be overlapped at the corner. Stitch through all thicknesses, as close to the cord as possible, using a zipper foot attachment.

2. Clip the corners and curves, turn the piping outward, and press the seam allowances to the wrong side of the aida cloth. Tack the piping ends to the seam allowance.

Figure C

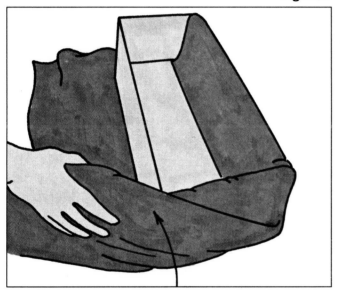

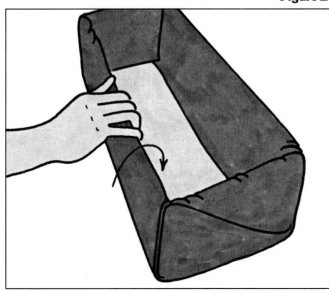

Covering the tray

1. The cross-stitched label will be attached to the calico fabric, which will then be used to cover the tray. To determine where the label should go, place the fabric wrong side up on a flat surface and place the tray in the center. Fold the fabric up around one long side of the tray, hold the label in the center, and mark the corner points with a pencil or straight pins. Remove the tray and whipstitch the label to the right side of the fabric.

2. The raw edges of the calico fabric can be finished in one of two ways. The simplest is to cut along each edge using pinking shears. Alternately, you can press a ½-inch allowance to the wrong side of the fabric on each edge and stitch.

3. Replace the tray in the center of the fabric (on the wrong side). Fold the front portion (with the label) up and over the edge of the tray, and glue the edge inside the tray. (Be sure the placement of the label is correct before glueing. If you are working with white glue, use clothespins or clamps to hold the glued fabric while it dries.

4. On one short end of the tray, fold the front portion of the fabric straight backward (**Figure C**) and glue it to the end and back of the tray on the outside. Fold the upper edge over the edge of the tray and glue it inside.

5. Pull the side of the fabric upward over the tray. The folded edge will reach from corner to corner across the end of the tray (**Figure D**). Glue the fabric inside the tray.

6. Repeat steps 4 and 5, working on the opposite end of the tray.

7. Fold the fabric up and over the long back side of the tray. Tuck the excess fabric underneath, so that the folded edges lie straight up and down along the corners (**Figure E**). Glue the fabric inside the tray.

8. If your tray is made of cardboard, line it with plastic or foil. Glue or tape the lining material inside the tray, over the bottom and about 2 inches up the sides. In addition to protecting the cardboard, this will prevent the fabric from acting like a wick and soaking up any water overflow.

9. Place the potted herbs inside, and your fashionable herb garden is ready to grace the kitchen window.

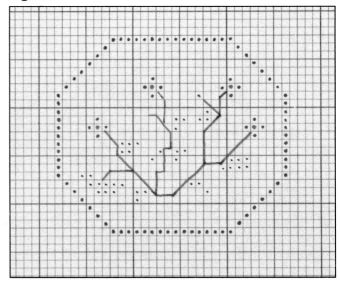

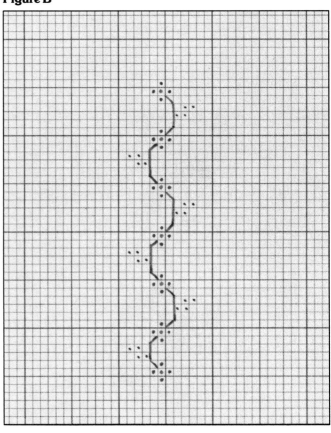

Book Cover and Bookmark

This patchwork book cover will accommodate the average paperback, and has handles for easy toting. It features a center panel with a cross-stitched motif that is repeated on the bookmark. This is a perfect gift item for your friends who enjoy reading books with no redeeming social value, but who are embarrassed to take them out in public.

Materials

A total of ½ yard of cotton fabric. We used small pieces of two different calicos and a larger amount of pin-dot fabric, all in shades of burgundy.

4 x 4-inch piece of ivory-colored 18-count aida cloth.

6-inch length of 1½- or 2-inch-wide cross-stitch ribbon, bound on both edges.

Embroidery floss in green, burgundy, and pink in shades to coordinate with the fabric.

11½ x 9-inch piece of thin quilt batting.

Burgundy sewing thread, needle, tapestry needle, sewing machine, steam iron, pins, scissors, pinking shears (optional), and measuring tape.

Cross-stitch

A color-coded cross-stitch graph for the center panel of the book cover is provided in **Figure A**. Stitch the design in the center of the 18-count aida cloth.

A graph for the bookmark design is given in **Figure B**. Work the design down the center of the cross-stitch ribbon. Hem the upper and lower ends of the ribbon, and your bookmark is complete!

Figure C

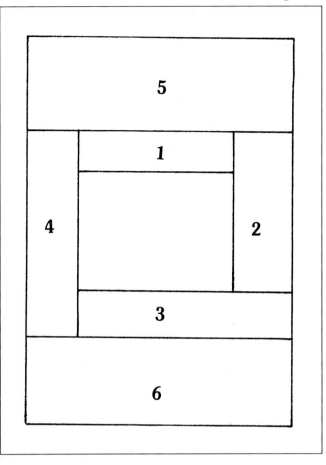

Cutting the pieces

A diagram of the front patchwork design is given in **Figure C.** (The numbers on the pieces refer to the order in which they will be assembled.) Fabric and cutting dimensions for each piece are listed below.

First calico fabric:
  patchwork piece 1 – 3¾ x 2 inches
  patchwork piece 2 – 4½ x 2 inches
  two handles – each 8 x 2 inches

Second calico fabric:
  patchwork piece 3 – 4¾ x 2 inches
  patchwork piece 4 – 5½ x 2 inches

Pin-dot fabric:
  border pieces 5 and 6 – each 5¾ x 2¾ inches
  back cover – 6¾ x 9 inches
  inner lining – 6 x 9 inches
  two inner flaps – each 5½ x 9 inches

Making the patchwork front

Note: All seam allowances are ½ inch.

1. Begin by assembling the patchwork front. Cut the cross-stitched aida cloth panel to 3¾ x 3½ inches (width x height), and staystitch ¼ inch from all edges.

2. Pin patchwork piece 1 along the upper edge of the aida cloth, placing right sides together. Stitch the seam and press it open (**Figure D**).

Figure D

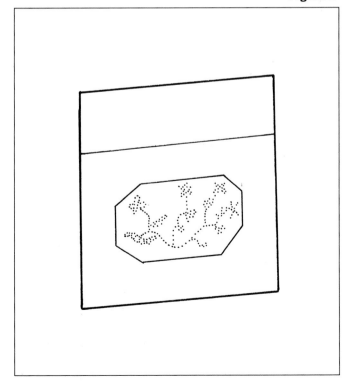

Figure E

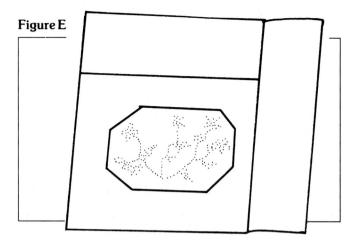

Figure F

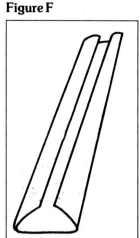

Figure G

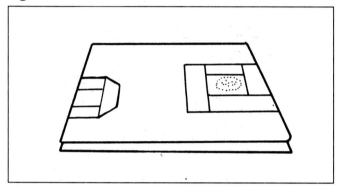

Figure H

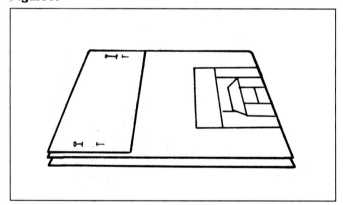

Figure I

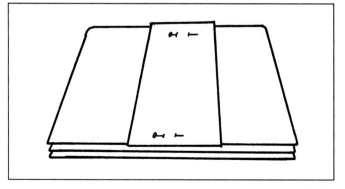

3. Pin patchwork piece 2 along the right-hand edge of the aida cloth and first strip, placing the right sides together. Stitch and press open (**Figure E**).

4. Follow the same procedures to attach piece 3 to the lower edge, and piece 4 to the left-hand edge. Stitch pieces 5 and 6 to the upper and lower edges of the resulting patchwork square. Refer back to the diagram given in **Figure C** if you become confused as to the order of assembly.

Assembling the cover

1. To join the front and back cover pieces, place one 9-inch edge of the pin-dot back cover along the left-hand edge of the patchwork front cover, right sides together. Stitch the seam and press open.

2. To prepare each handle, press a ¼-inch allowance to the wrong side along each long edge (**Figure F**). Fold the handle in half lengthwise, wrong sides together, and press. Stitch through all thicknesses, close to the turned edges, using a widely-spaced zigzag setting.

3. The inner lining and flaps also need a little preparation before assembly. Pink the two 9-inch edges of the inner lining (or stitch using a zigzag setting), to keep them from fraying. On each inner flap, turn a ½-inch allowance to the wrong side on one 9-inch edge, and press. Run a line of widely-spaced zigzag stitches close to the turned edge.

4. Place the quilt batting on a flat surface. Pin the assembled cover on top, right side up (**Figure G**). Fold one handle into a horseshoe shape and pin the raw ends even with the edge of the cover and batting on one side as shown. Pin the remaining handle to the opposite side in the same manner, and baste close to all four edges.

5. Pin one inner flap over the cover and handle on one side, placing right sides together, as shown in **Figure H**. Pin the remaining flap over the handle on the opposite side. Center the inner lining over the entire assembly, right side down (**Figure I**), and pin it along the upper and lower edges. Stitch a continuous seam around all four edges, through all layers (batting, cover, handles, flaps, and inner lining). Clip the four corners.

6. To turn the assembly right side out, first turn the inner lining to the batting side, then turn each of the flaps. Press gently, insert the current best-seller, and settle down for a fashionable read!

Soft Treasure Boxes

Every young lady needs a special place to keep her most treasured possessions. A soft frilly box is just the thing.

Materials

The basic materials needed to make one box are:

¾ yard of 36-inch-wide fabric. (We made boxes from several different fabrics, and discovered that a medium-weight fabric with body like corduroy works best. If you use a light-weight fabric, we suggest that you back it with a stiff interfacing material.)

1¼ yards of 1½-inch-wide white eyelet trim.

1 yard of ¾-inch-wide woven ribbon-and-lace trim or a yard of 1-inch-wide eyelet. (As you can see from the three boxes pictured here, there are lots of different ways you can decorate the box top. So you may wish to purchase additional trims.)

6 x 10-inch piece of ivory-colored 11-count aida cloth.

17 x 21-inch piece of 6-ply quilt batting, bonded on at least one side.

Embroidery floss in two or three colors to coordinate with the fabric and trims.

8 x 12-inch piece of cardboard.

Tapestry and regular needles, thread to match the fabric, sewing machine, pattern paper, scissors, pins, and a steam iron.

Cross-stitch

We created two different cross-stitch designs for the box tops. Both are pictured here. As you can see, one design consists of a running horse, a name, and a border. The other design consists of a name with flowers and a border.

You'll find a cross-stitch graph for the horse in **Figure A**. Stitch the horse slightly above the center of the aida cloth, to accommodate the name below.

An alphabet graph (including the flower design) is provided in **Figure B.** Cross-stitch a name below the horse or, for the second design, in the center of the cloth. Stitch a flower at each side of the name.

To make the border, simply work a complete cross-stitch over every second thread (skipping one space between each stitch), all the way around the center design.

Figure A

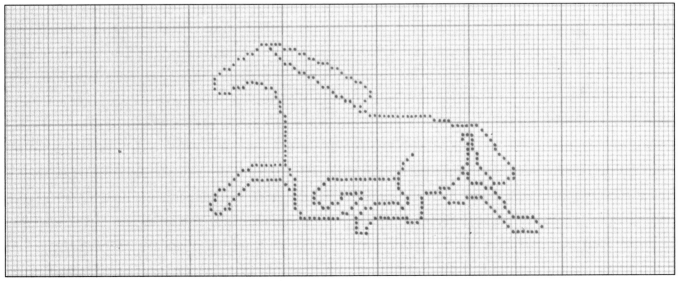

Figure B

Figure C　　　　　　　　　　　　　　　　　1 sq. = 1 inch

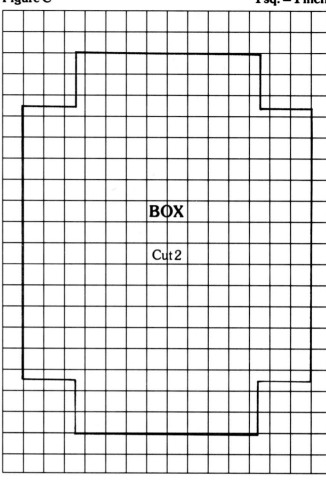

BOX

Cut 2

Figure D

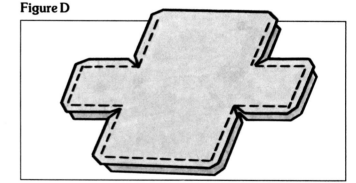

Figure E

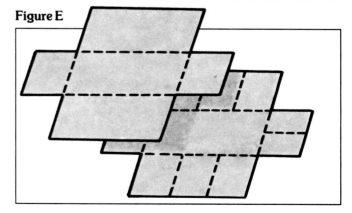

Making the box

Note: All seam allowances are ½ inch.

1. A scale drawing for the box pattern is given in **Figure C**. Enlarge the drawing to a full-size paper pattern.

2. Cut two box pieces from your chosen fabric. Try to cut (and later stitch) very straight lines so you'll have a neat, well-fitting box and lid.

3. Pin the two fabric box pieces right sides together and stitch the seam around all edges, leaving one long edge open and unstitched. Clip the seam allowances at all corners as shown (**Figure D**). Turn the box right side out and press gently. Turn the seam allowances to the inside on the two remaining raw edges, and press.

4. Use the stitched fabric box as a pattern to cut a piece of quilt batting. Insert the cut batting between the two fabric layers of the box, working it into the corners until it lies smoothly in place. Whipstitch the opening edges together.

5. Topstitch through all layers of the box along the fold lines, as shown in **Figure E**. (As an optional step, you can also topstitch along the lines illustrated in the second drawing, **Figure E**, for a quilted effect.) Fold the sides up and whipstitch them together along the corner seams (**Figure F**).

Figure F

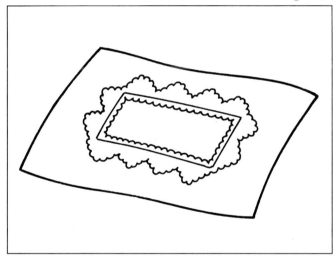

Figure G

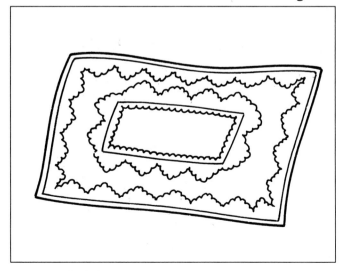

Figure H

Making the box top

1. First, prepare the cross-stitched aida cloth by pressing the seam allowance to the wrong side on each edge.

2. Cut a lid piece and a lining piece, each 9 x 13 inches, from your chosen fabric. Place the lid piece right side up on a flat surface. Pin the cross-stitched aida cloth, right side up, in the center of the lid. Topstitch ¼ inch from each edge.

3. Pin a length of woven ribbon-and-lace trim (or narrow eyelet) over the edges of the aida cloth (**Figure G**), beginning and ending at a lower corner and folding the raw ends of the lace underneath. Topstitch in place. You may wish to stitch additional lace, eyelet, or fabric borders to the lid, as we did for some of the boxes pictured.

4. Pin the length of wide eyelet around the raw edges of the fabric lid, as shown in **Figure H**. The bound edge of the eyelet should be even with the raw edges of the fabric, and the scalloped eyelet edge should extend in toward the center. Make a generous pleat of eyelet at each corner, so it will not be stretched flat when it is turned outward. Baste the eyelet in place.

5. Pin the lid lining right side down over the lid (the cross-stitch and trims will be sandwiched between). Stitch the seams along both short side edges and the long front edge, leaving the long rear edge open and unstitched. Clip the corners, turn the lid right side out, and press gently.

6. Turn the seam allowances to the inside on the two remaining raw edges, and press. Use the stitched lid as a pattern to cut a piece of quilt batting and a piece of cardboard. Insert the cardboard and batting between the lid and lining, with the batting on top. Whipstitch the opening edges together.

7. Place the finished lid over the box, and whipstitch them together along the long back edge.

8. If you like, add a satin ribbon bow or other finishing touch to the decorated lid.

Festive Door Wreath

This colorful door wreath is full of wonderful surprises — pinecones, silk greenery, dried flowers, and cross-stitched fruit!

Materials

⅝ yard of medium-weight dark green fabric.

Fifteen medium-size pinecones.

One bunch of dried baby's breath.

Green silk leaves. We used about 30 three-leaf clusters, called artificial rose leaves.

2 yards of 3-inch-wide lace-edged purple satin ribbon.

15-inch-diameter styrofoam wreath base, with a center opening about 7 inches in diameter.

19-inch square of quilt batting.

Small amount of polyester fiberfill.

For each cross-stitched apple, you'll need a 4 x 4½-inch piece of red 14-count aida cloth and a piece of medium-weight fabric of the same size in a coordinating color for the back. We made two apples.

For each pear, you'll need a 4 x 5-inch piece of pale green 14-count aida cloth and a coordinating piece of fabric for the back. We made two pears.

For each cluster of cherries, you'll need a 4 x 4-inch piece of deep pink 14-count aida cloth, and a coordinating piece of fabric for the back. We made four cherry clusters.

For each banana, you'll need a 4 x 11-inch piece of yellow 14-count aida cloth, and a coordinating piece of fabric for the back. We made two bananas.

Embroidery floss in brown, fuchsia, pale pink, deep yellow, pale yellow, gold, and charcoal gray.

Thread to match the fabrics, regular and tapestry needles, pins, scissors, glue gun and hot-melt adhesive (or white glue), steam iron, sewing machine.

CHERRIES
Brown ●
Fuchsia ·
Pale Pink X

PEAR
Grey ●
Deep Yellow X
Pale Yellow ·

APPLE
Brown ●
Fuchsia ·
Pale Pink X

Figure A

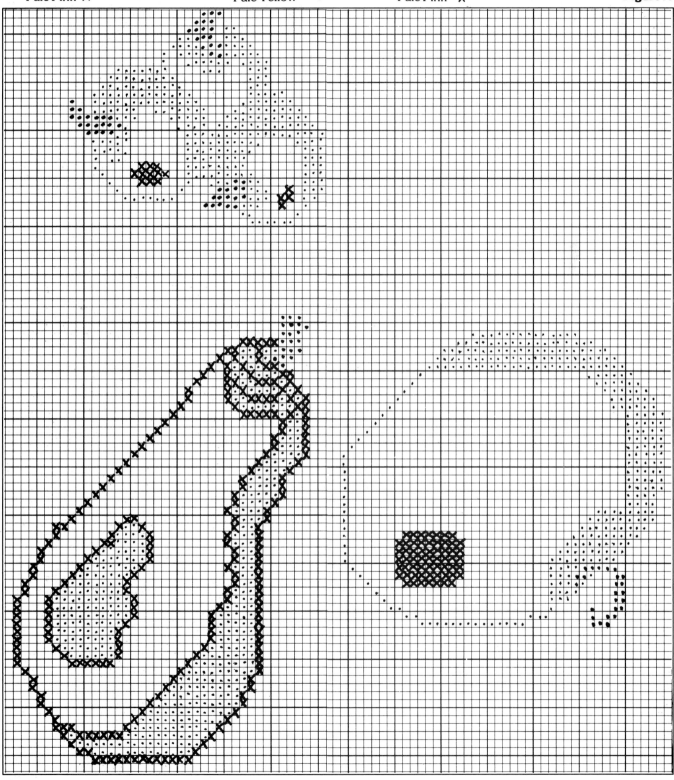

Figure A

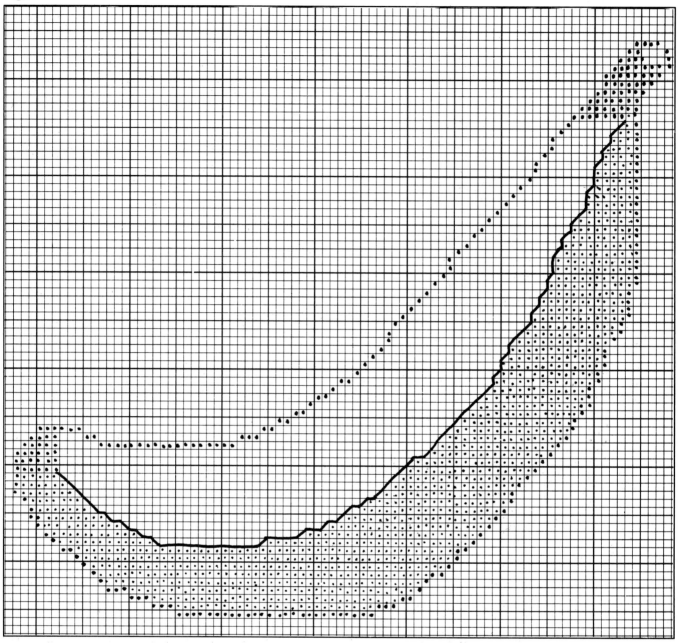

BANANA
Brown —
Gold ·
Brown ●

Cross-stitch

Color-coded cross-stitch graphs for the apple, pear, cherry cluster, and banana are provided in **Figure A**. We made two apples, two pears, four cherry clusters, and two bananas. Work the designs on the cloth specified in the materials list. Press all of the cross-stitch on the wrong side of the fabric, using a steam setting.

Assembling the fruit

1. Cut each piece of aida cloth to the shape of the fruit, leaving an extra ⅝ inch allowance all the way around the cross-stitched outline.

2. Cut a back piece for each fruit, using the shaped aida cloth piece as a pattern.

3. For each fruit, pin the aida cloth and back pieces right sides together. Stitch a ½-inch-wide seam around the outer edge, leaving a 2-inch opening. Clip the corners and turn the stitched fruit right side out through the opening. Press the seam allowances to the inside along the opening edges.

4. Stuff the fruit with fiberfill, and whipstitch the opening edges together.

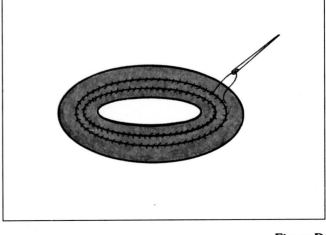

Figure C

Figure B

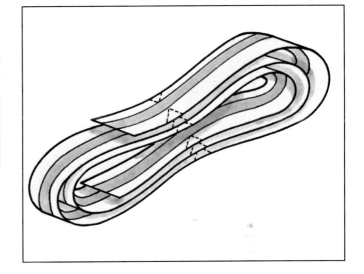

Figure D

Covering the wreath base

1. To cut a back cover piece, place the styrofoam base on the wrong side of the green fabric and trace the outer and inner outlines of the base on the fabric. Cut away the excess fabric ⅜ inch outside the larger circle and ⅜ inch inside the smaller circle (**Figure B**). Clip the curves and press a ½-inch allowance to the wrong side of the fabric on both circular raw edges. Topstitch close to each turned edge.

2. To make a front cover piece, trace the outer and inner base outlines on the wrong side of the remaining green fabric. Cut away the excess fabric 2 inches outside the larger circle and 2 inches inside the smaller circle. Clip the curves and press a ½-inch allowance to the wrong side of the fabric around both circular edges.

3. Use the front cover piece as a pattern to cut the quilt batting. Clip the curve around the inner circle on the batting, and glue the batting to the front of the styrofoam base, wrapping the edges to the back. If you are using white glue, pin the batting in place while the glue dries.

4. Place the back cover piece against the back of the wreath base and pin it in a few places to secure it temporarily. Place the front cover piece against the front of the base (over the batting) and wrap the edges around to the back, over the edges of the back cover piece. Pin the front cover piece to the back cover piece and whipstitch around the outer and inner edges (**Figure C**).

Decorating the wreath

Decorate the front of the covered wreath base in a manner that is pleasing to you, glueing the various materials in place. (If you use white glue instead of hot-melt adhesive, you'll find that the heavier materials will not stay attached for very long. In that case, we suggest that you tack the pieces to the fabric, or wire them to floral picks and insert the picks through the cover, into the styrofoam.) We started with a base of rose leaves and then added clusters of pinecones, leaving spaces for the cross-stitched fruits and a large space for the bow. The dried baby's breath can be used to fill in after the other materials have been attached.

To make the bow, first cut an 18-inch length of the wide ribbon to use as a center tie. Wrap the remaining length of ribbon loosely around a book or other object to form a series of double-ended loops, each about 9 inches long. Flatten the loops in the center and cut a notch into each side (**Figure D**). Wrap the center tie around the loops at the notches, tie it tightly at the back, and cut the ends at an angle. Spread and twist the loops of the bow into an attractive arrangement.

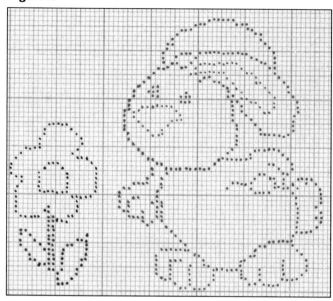

Easter Basket

This delightful basket will hold lots of eggs and candy, and is guaranteed to delight any child. It can also be used as a table centerpiece or Easter decoration anywhere in the house.

Materials

¾ yard of 14-count ivory-colored aida cloth, at least 36 inches wide.

1½ yards of pastel plaid fabric, 36 inches wide.

1 yard of ivory-colored single-fold nylon braid, ½ inch wide.

1 yard of ivory-colored 1-inch-wide eyelet trim.

1½ yards of ½-inch-wide light blue satin ribbon, and 1½ yards of purple.

Light-weight cardboard: one circular piece 9¼ inches in diameter, and one rectangular piece 5½ x 28 inches.

One piece of bonded quilt batting, 5½ x 26½ inches.

Embroidery floss in blue, pink, purple, and green.

Tapestry and regular needles, scissors, pins, sewing machine, and iron.

Cross-stitch

A graph for the cross-stitch Easter bunny and flower design is given in **Figure A**. Cut a 7½ x 27½-inch piece of aida cloth for the basket side, and work the design in the center. We worked the flower in purple, the leaves in green, the bunny in blue, and the bunny's ears and nose in pink. Press the cloth gently on the wrong side, using a steam setting.

Making the basket

Note: All seam allowances are ½ inch unless otherwise specified in the instructions.

1. The cross-stitched aida will serve as the sides of the basket. Cut the following additional pieces from the aida cloth: three straps, each 2 x 36 inches; and one circular bottom, 9½ inches in diameter.

2. Cut the following pieces from the pastel plaid fabric: one side lining, 6 x 27½ inches; one circular bottom lining, 8 inches in diameter; and one strap, 5 x 25 inches. In addition, cut and piece together 8-inch-wide strips to form one continuous strip, 8 x 80 inches. This will be the ruffle.

3. Fold the plaid ruffle piece in half lengthwise, placing wrong sides together, and press. Press the seam allowances to the inside on both short ends. Gather the long raw edges just inside the seam line, using long basting stitches. Pin the gathered edge of the ruffle along one long edge of the side lining piece, on the right side of the fabric. Adjust the gathers evenly, so that the ruffle fits between the side seam allowances of the lining and baste (**Figure B**).

4. Pin the cross-stitched aida cloth right side down over the ruffle and lining, placing the top of the bunny's head toward the seam. Stitch the seam along the ruffle edge. Press the seam open.

5. Fold this assembly in half widthwise, placing right sides together, and stitch the seam along the short raw edges (**Figure C**). Be sure not to catch the ends of the ruffle in the seam. Press the seam open.

6. Pin the plaid bottom lining inside the open edge of the plaid side lining, placing right sides together and easing the lining to fit. Stitch the seam (**Figure D**). Clip the curves.

7. Turn the aida cloth right side out, folding it over the lining so that the ruffle is on the top edge. Topstitch through all thicknesses, just below the ruffle (**Figure E**).

8. Insert the cardboard rectangle between the aida and lining layers, overlapping the ends. Insert the batting rectangle between the cardboard and the lining.

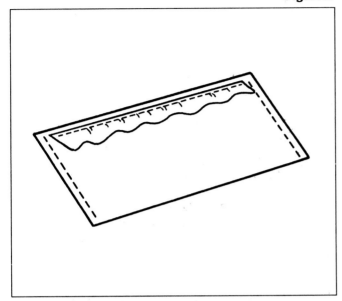

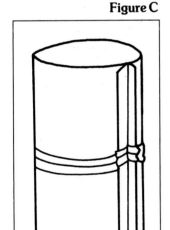

Figure C

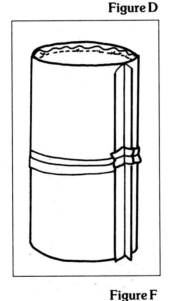

Figure D

Figure E

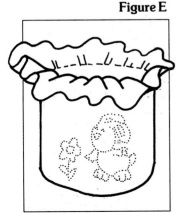

Figure F

Adding the Basket Bottom

1. Place the aida cloth bottom piece on a flat surface. Glue the cardboard circle to the center of the cloth. Clip the lower raw edge of the aida cloth basket side ½ inch deep at 2-inch intervals. Place the basket in the center of the cardboard circle, flaring the clipped edge outward, and adjusting the edges of the two aida layers to fit (**Figure F**). Pin and then stitch the aida layers together, ¼ inch from the edge.

2. Encase and glue the raw edges of the aida layers inside the single-fold nylon braid, beginning and ending at the vertical seam in the back of the basket. Glue the eyelet trim around the bottom of the basket so that it covers the clipping.

Making the Strap

1. Fold one aida cloth strap piece in half lengthwise, and stitch the seam along the long raw edges. Repeat for the remaining two strap pieces. Turn the straps right sides out and press.

2. Tack the three straps together at one end and braid the entire length to form a flat braid.

3. Fold the plaid strap in half lengthwise, right sides together. Stitch the seam along one short end and the long raw edges. Turn the strap right side out, and press the seam allowances to the inside on the remaining raw edges. Whipstitch the open edges together.

4. Whipstitch the braided strap to the center length of the plaid strap, beginning and ending even with the ends of the fabric. Trim the braid to fit if necessary.

5. Attach the assembled strap to the basket with the ends flush at the bottom, securely whipstitching the fabric strap to the lining.

6. Tie the ribbons around the basket just underneath the ruffle, ending with a bow in the front.

7. Wait for the Easter Bunny.

Family Portrait

It won't be hard getting the family together for this portrait because it's done by you in cross-stitch. The design can be adapted to any size family.

Materials

Note: The materials listed are for a family of four: mother, father, girl and boy. You will need to adjust the amount of materials depending on the number of people in your family.

1½ yards of red-and-white pin-dot fabric.
1 yard of red cotton fabric with a small pattern.
1¾ yards of double-fold beige bias binding, ¾ inch wide.
9¼ x 18¼-inch piece of ivory-colored 14-count aida cloth.
3½ x 4-inch piece of dark brown aida cloth.
12 x 21-inch ceiling tile, or substitute ⅜-inch-thick plywood.
Embroidery floss in light blue, brown, flesh tone, green, navy blue, red, and yellow.
Two green silk leaves, each 2 inches long.
⅝ yard of ⅛-inch-wide pink satin ribbon.
4-inch length of ½-inch-wide eyelet trim.
Small remnants of lace trim and fabric.
Two tiny yellow beads.
Tapestry and regular needles, scissors, sewing machine, pins, graph paper, pencil, measuring tape, glue, and stapler.

Cross-stitch

It will be necessary to draw your own cross-stitch graph before starting this project, in order to place your family figures and names correctly. Stitching graphs for the heart and for all letters of the alphabet are provided in **Figure A**. Color-coded graphs for individual characters (mother, father, boy, and girl) are given in **Figure B**. Be sure to include the heart, and leave space for the fabric flowerpot on your graph.

Stitch your entire family, working from your graph. Place the first names below the figures. Stitch the heart in the center, and stitch your family name inside the heart. We used red floss for the heart and for the first names, and blue for the last name.

78

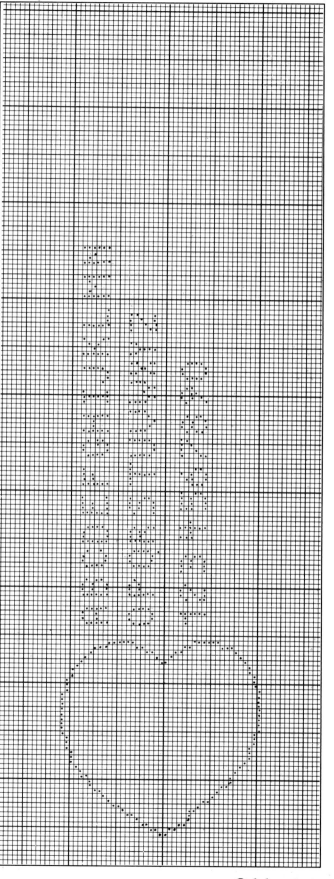

Celebrations

Dressing the family

1. For each little girl in your portrait, cut a 2-inch length of lace trim and glue it across the bottom of the dress. Cut four pieces of ⅛-inch-wide ribbon, each 4 inches long, and tie four tiny bows. Glue a bow at the end of each pigtail, and one on each shoe.

2. For the father and each little boy, cut a 1-inch square of scrap fabric and press a ⅛-inch hem to the wrong side on all four edges. Glue the square to the center of the overall bib. Cut short lengths of brown embroidery floss, tie them in tiny bows, and stitch them to the shoes as shoelaces.

3. For the mother, cut fabric or bias tape to make the belt for her dress. Turn the ends under and glue them in place. Glue two small beads at her neckline and sew a yellow floss ribbon in her hair.

Flowerpot

Note: All seam allowances are ½ inch.

1. A full-size pattern for the flowerpot is given in **Figure C**. Cut one pot from brown aida cloth, placing the center of the pot along a fold. Press a ½-inch hem allowance to the wrong side on all edges.

Figure C

Figure B

Place on fold

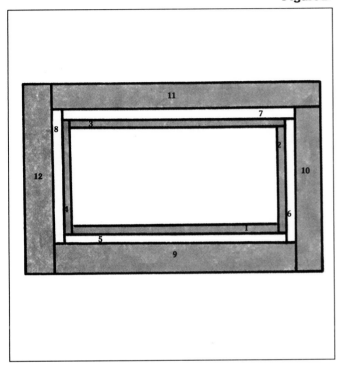

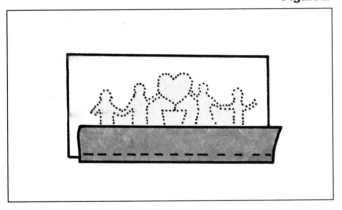

Cutting the frame pieces

A diagram of the log-cabin patchwork frame is given in **Figure D**. The frame consists of three layers. On each layer, piecing begins at the bottom edge and continues counter-clockwise around the remaining edges. The numbers on the pieces refer to the order in which they are assembled.

The cutting dimensions for each piece are listed below. (Of course, if you have a larger or smaller picture, the sizes will be different.) Cut pieces 1 through 4 from pin-dot fabric; 5 through 8 from bias tape; and 9 through 12 from red patterned fabric.

Pieces 1 and 3 – each 7 x 19 inches
Pieces 2 and 4 – each 7 x 11 inches
Pieces 5 and 7 – each 20 inches
Pieces 6 and 8 – each 12 inches
Pieces 9 and 11 – each 5 x 25½ inches
Pieces 10 and 12 – each 5 x 21½ inches

Making the log-cabin frame

1. Place the cross-stitched aida cloth right side up on a flat surface. The first layer of the frame is pin-dot fabric. Place Piece 1 right side down over the aida cloth, with lower edges even. Pin and then stitch the seam along the lower edge (**Figure E**). Turn the frame piece outward and press the seam allowances toward the frame. Trim the ends even with the aida cloth.

2. Place Piece 2 right side down over the aida cloth and Piece 1. Pin and then stitch the seam along the right-hand edge. Turn the frame piece outward and press the seam allowances toward the frame. Trim the ends.

3. Complete the first layer, attaching Piece 3 to the upper edge and Piece 4 to the left-hand edge following the procedures described in steps 1 and 2.

4. Add the second frame layer (Pieces 5 through 8, which are lengths of bias binding). Place each piece, in sequence, ¼ inch from the folded inner edge of the pin-dot frame, and topstitch close to the outer edge.

5. Pieces 9 through 12 form the final layer of the frame. Place Piece 9 right side down over the aida cloth, so that one long edge is even with the lower edge of the second (bias binding) frame layer. Stitch the seam, press the frame piece outward, and trim the ends. Follow the same procedures to attach the remaining frame pieces in sequence to the edges of the assembly.

Final assembly

Center the aida cloth on the ceiling tile or plywood. Glue or staple the edges of the frame fabric to the back of the tile, folding the corners neatly.

2. Glue the eyelet trim just below the rim of the pot, folding the raw ends to the wrong side of the brown fabric. Cut a 4-inch length of ⅛-inch-wide ribbon and glue it on top of the eyelet, folding the ends to the wrong side.

3. Glue or whipstitch the sides and bottom of the flower pot to the aida cloth about 1¼ inches beneath the heart. Do not attach the upper edge at this time.

4. Glue the two green leaves and the stem to the aida cloth under the top edge of the flowerpot, so that the heart becomes the blossom.

5. Glue or whipstitch the top edge of the flowerpot to the aida cloth.

Celebrations

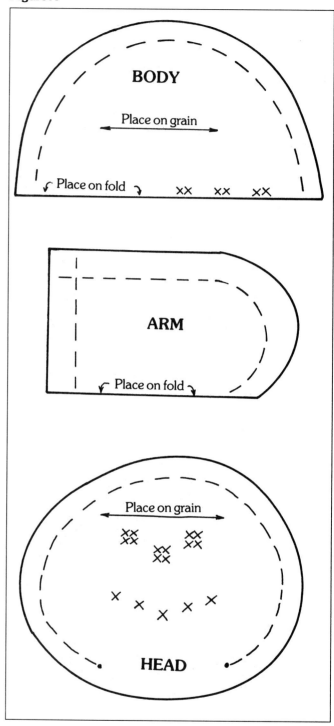

Cross-Stitch Christmas Ornaments

These three cross-stitched Christmas characters will add a touch of homespun charm to your tree. Each carries a goodie bag that will hold candy or other small holiday treats.

Materials

You'll need the following supplies or tools for each of the ornaments. Additional materials required for each separate ornament are specified with the individual instructions.

White glue, small quantity of polyester fiberfill, heavy-duty white, red, and black threads, regular sewing needle, tapestry needle, sewing machine (optional), scissors, pins, iron. If you have a hot-melt glue gun, use it instead of white glue — it will make the work go faster and hold better. Otherwise, pin the glued pieces until they are dry.

Cross-stitch

Each ornament has cross-stitched details. Stitching graphs showing these details are provided on the full-size patterns. An alphabet graph is also provided. You will be working from this graph to stitch the words "JOY" and "GOODIES" which appear on the bags. If you wish, add a name or (necessarily short) holiday message to any of the ornaments.

NOTE: On each full-size pattern, you will see a long, double-ended arrow. Be sure that the arrow lies along the straight grain of the fabric when cutting. This is particularly important for the pieces that will be cross-stitched, otherwise your stitches will look cockeyed.

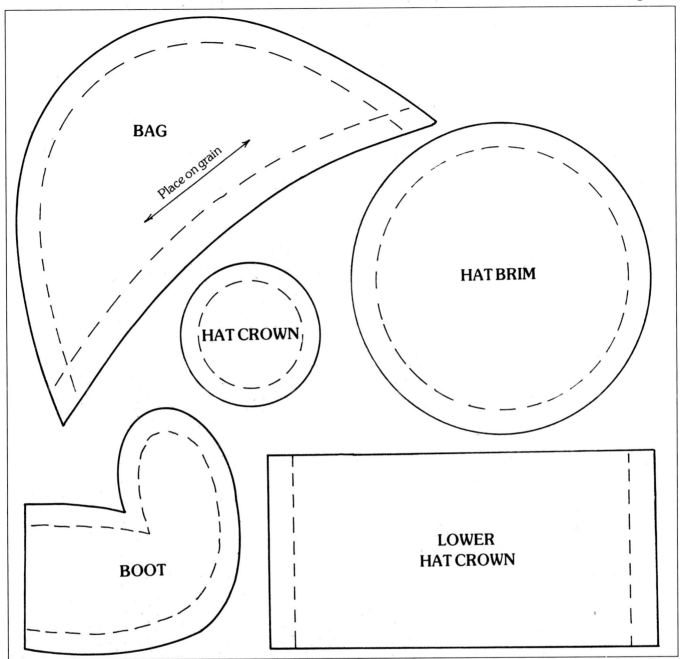

Snowman materials

8 x 10-inch piece of white 14-count aida cloth.

5½ x 5½-inch piece of red 14-count aida cloth.

7 x 11-inch piece of black cotton fabric.

5½ x 5½-inch piece of red-and-white polka-dot fabric (or any other design) for the bag lining.

Small scraps of red and green felt.

12-inch length of ⅛-inch-wide white satin ribbon.

12-inch length of ¾-inch-wide red-and-green plaid ribbon.

Small quantities of black and white embroidery floss.

One red-headed straight pin (optional).

Making the body

1. Cut two each of the body, head, and arm from white aida cloth, using the full-size patterns provided in **Figure A**.

2. Cross-stitch graphs for the facial features and front buttons are provided on the head and body patterns. Using black embroidery floss, cross-stitch the facial features on one of the aida cloth head pieces, and the buttons on one body piece.

Figure B

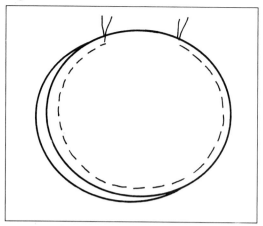

Figure C

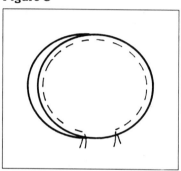

Figure D

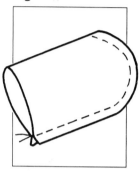

Figure E

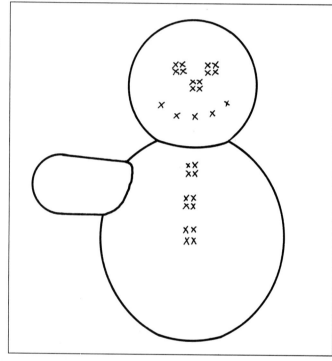

Figure F

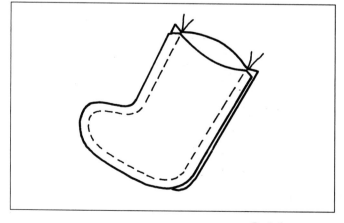

3. Place the two body pieces right sides together and stitch close to the edge, leaving a 1½-inch-long opening at the top (**Figure B**). Clip the curves, turn the body right side out, and stuff gently with fiberfill. Turn the raw edges to the inside along the opening, and press.

4. Place the two heads right sides together and stitch close to the long curved edge, leaving the neck edge open and unstitched (**Figure C**). Clip the curve, turn the stitched head right side out, press gently, and stuff. Whipstitch the neck opening together.

5. Pin the whipstitched neck edge of the head inside the neck opening of the body, with the cross-stitched designs facing the front, and whipstitch them securely together around the neck.

6. Fold one aida cloth arm in half (**Figure D**), right sides together, and stitch close to the long raw edge, leaving the straight shoulder edge open and unstitched. Clip the curve, turn the stitched arm right side out, and press. Stuff the hand portion lightly. Leave the upper arm unstuffed. Turn the raw edges to the inside and press. Glue or whipstitch the arm to the body (**Figure E**). Repeat for the second arm.

7. Cut four boot pieces from black cotton fabric. Place two boot pieces right sides together and stitch around the edges, leaving the straight upper edge open and unstitched (**Figure F**). Clip the curve, turn the stitched boot right side out, press, and stuff. Turn the raw upper edges to the inside of the stuffed boot and press. Glue or whipstitch the boot to the lower edge of the body, pointing the toes to the front. Repeat for the second boot, using the remaining two boot pieces.

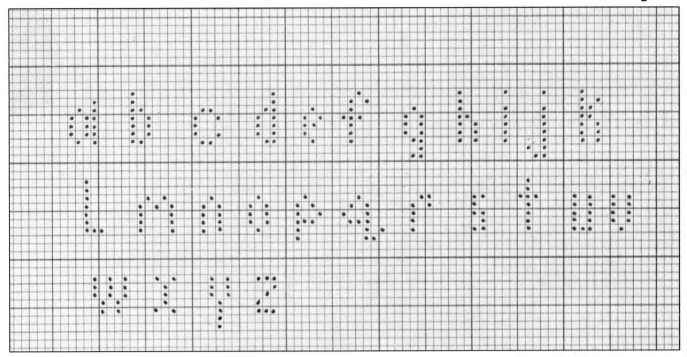

Figure H

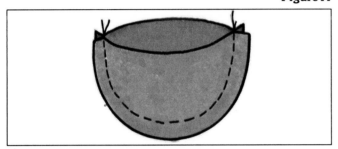

Figure J

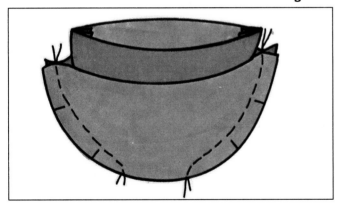

Figure I

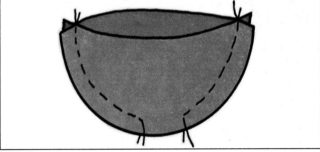

2. Cross-stitch "JOY" in the center of one aida cloth bag, referring to the alphabet graph provided in **Figure G**. Use white floss.

3. Place the two aida cloth bag pieces right sides together and stitch close to the long curved edge, leaving the upper edge open and unstitched (**Figure H**). Clip the curve. Place the two polka-dot lining pieces right sides together, and stitch as you did the outer bag, but leave a 1½-inch opening at the bottom of the curve (**Figure I**). Clip the curve in several places.

4. Turn the aida cloth bag right side out and slip it inside the stitched lining, which should still be wrong side out (**Figure J**), so that the upper raw edges are even. Stitch the lining to the outer bag around the entire upper edge. Turn the assembly right side out through the opening at the bottom of the lining, and then whipstitch the opening together. Gently push the lining down inside the outer bag and press.

5. Temporarily pin the assembled bag to the front of the Snowman, just below the lowest cross-stitched button. Fold the arms forward and tack each hand to one side of the goodie bag.

Making the bag

1. A full-size pattern for the bag is provided in **Figure A**. Cut two bag pieces from red aida cloth, and two additional bag pieces from the red-and-white polka-dot lining fabric.

Celebrations

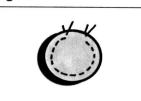

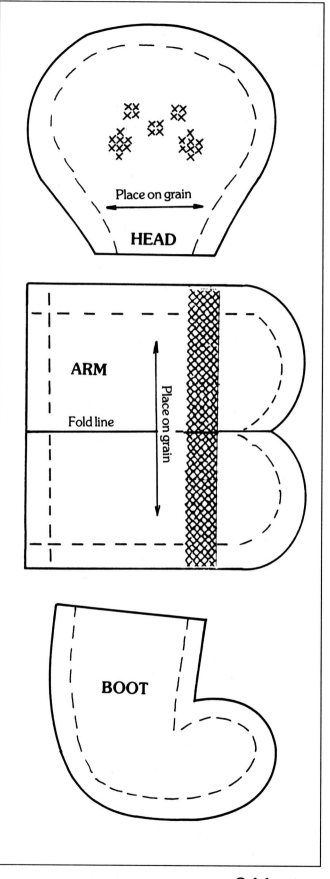

HEAD

Place on grain

ARM

Fold line

Place on grain

BOOT

Adding the hat and details

1. Full-size hat patterns are provided in **Figure A**. Cut one upper crown, one lower crown, and two brim pieces from black cotton fabric.

2. Staystitch ¼ inch from each long edge of the lower crown piece. Fold the piece in half widthwise, right sides together, and stitch the seam close to the raw edge (**Figure L**). Turn the lower crown right side out, and press the seam allowances to the wrong side around the upper and lower edges, along the staystitching.

3. Staystitch close to the raw edge all the way around the crown piece. Clip the curve in several places, and press the allowance to the wrong side along the staystitching. Glue or whipstitch the upper crown over one end of the lower crown.

4. Stitch the two brim pieces right sides together around the entire raw edge, leaving a 1-inch opening (**Figure K**). Clip the curve in several places, turn right side out through the opening, and press. Whipstitch the opening together. Glue or whipstitch the assembled crown to the center of the brim.

5. Cut a ¼-inch-wide strip of red felt and glue it around the lower edge of the crown as a hatband, overlapping the ends at the back. Cut a small piece of green felt in the shape of a holly leaf, and glue it to the hatband. Add a round red berry cut from felt (or a red-headed pin).

6. Glue or whipstitch the assembled hat to the Snowman's head at a jaunty angle. Bend the brim downward at the front and glue or stitch in place.

7. Tie the length of red-and-green plaid ribbon around the Snowman's neck as a muffler.

8. To form the hanging loop, fold the length of narrow white ribbon in half and knot the ends together. Whipstitch the knotted ends of the loop to the back of the Snowman's head, below the hat brim. In addition, tack the ribbon to the hat just above the hatband, so that the ornament will hang vertically.

Santa Materials

8 x 10-inch piece of 14-count red aida cloth.
3 x 6-inch piece of 14-count pale pink aida cloth.
7 x 10-inch piece of black fabric.
Small scraps of green and red felt.
White pompon, about 1 inch in diameter.
12-inch length of ⅛-inch-wide white satin ribbon.
Small skein of white yarn.
White, black, and deep pink embroidery floss.
Small artist's paint brush, pencil, or other long, thin, roundish
    object (to wrap the yarn around to make the curly hair).
One red-headed straight pin (optional).

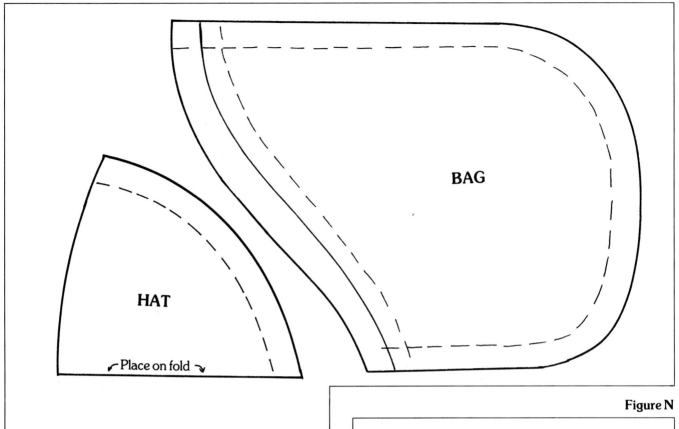

BAG

HAT

⌐Place on fold ⌐

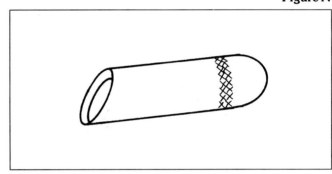

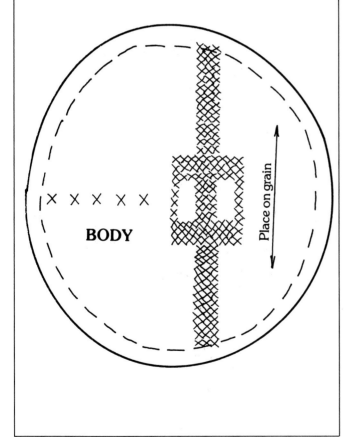

× × × × ×

BODY

Place on grain

Making the body

1. Using the full-size patterns provided in **Figure M**, cut two body pieces and two arm pieces from red aida cloth. Cut two head pieces from pink aida cloth, and four boot pieces from black cotton fabric.

2. Follow the stitching graphs provided to cross-stitch the facial features on one head piece, using pink for the nose and cheek spots, and black for the eyes. Cross-stitch the buttons and belt with buckle on one body piece, using black floss. Cross-stitch a black belt (no buckle) on the remaining body piece, and a white cuff at the end of each arm piece.

3. Stitch, turn, stuff, and assemble Santa's body, head, arms, and boots as described for the Snowman. (See "Making the body," steps 3 through 7 for the Snowman.) On step 6, turn the raw shoulder edges under on the diagonal (**Figure N**), so the arms will slant slightly upward when attached to the body.

Adding the hat, hair, and sack

1. Use the full-size hat pattern in **Figure M** to cut one hat piece from a double layer of red aida cloth, placing the pattern on a fold of the fabric. Without unfolding the fabric, stitch the back seam close to the raw edges (**Figure O**). Turn the stitched hat right side out.

2. Staystitch ¼ inch from the lower raw edge, and press the allowance to the wrong side along the staystitching. Stitch the white pompon to the point of the hat, and glue or whipstitch the hat to Santa's head at a slight angle. Cut a green felt holly leaf and add a red headed pin or felt holly berry. Glue them to the hat.

3. To make hair and beard, thread a needle with a generous length of heavy duty white thread. Take a stitch through one end of the white yarn, and anchor it to the back of Santa's stuffed head.

4. Starting where the yarn is anchored to the head, wrap the yarn eight or ten times around the shaft of a small paint brush (or other long, thin object). Insert the needle between the loops of yarn and the shaft at one end (**Figure P**), and push it out through the other end. Carefully remove the paint brush and take a stitch into the head near the first stitch. Pull the thread tightly to secure the curl.

5. Repeat this procedure to create curls on the back of the head below the hat, around the lower part of the face as a beard, and around the upper portion of the face and lower portion of the hat. Tack the end of the yarn firmly underneath the last curl.

6. Cut two sack pieces from black cotton fabric, using the full-size pattern in **Figure M**. Place them right sides together, and stitch close to the long contoured edge. Turn the stitched sack right side out. Press a narrow hem allowance to the wrong side around the upper raw edge, turn the hem under again, and topstitch in place.

7. Glue or whipstitch the longer corner of the sack over Santa's right shoulder. Fold the right arm forward, so that the hand covers the corner of the sack, and whipstitch or glue the hand in place.

8. To form the hanging loop, Fold the length of white satin ribbon in half and knot the ends together. Glue or whipstitch the knotted ends to the base of Santa's hat at the center back. Tack one side of the loop to the pompon at the top of the hat, so that Santa will hang straight (or "plumb," as they say in the trade).

Figure O

Figure P

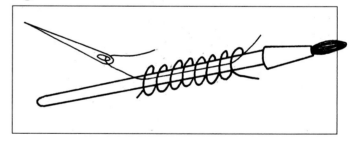

Mrs. Santa materials

7 x 8-inch piece of red 14-count aida cloth.
4 x 6-inch piece of pink 14-count aida cloth.
6 x 7-inch piece of ivory 14-count aida cloth.
6 x 6-inch piece of black cotton fabric.
1 x 5-inch piece of green-and-white polka-dot fabric (or other pattern) for the hat.
4 x 7-inch piece of red-and-white polka-dot fabric (or other pattern) for the goodie bag lining.
Small scraps of green and red felt.
8-inch length of white eyelet trim, approximately 1 inch wide.
Small skein of white yarn.
20-inch length of ⅛-inch-wide white satin ribbon.
Red pompon, approximately 1 inch in diameter.
White, black, deep pink, green, and red embroidery floss.
Small artist's paint brush, pencil, or other round object.
Two red-headed straight pins (optional).

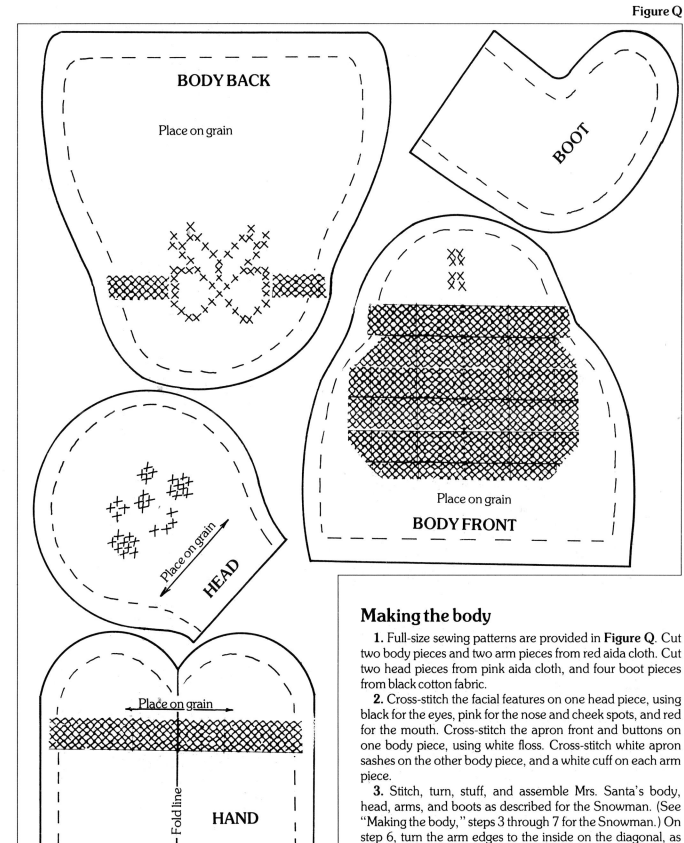

BODY BACK

Place on grain

BOOT

BODY FRONT

Place on grain

HEAD

Place on grain

HAND

Place on grain

Fold line

Making the body

1. Full-size sewing patterns are provided in **Figure Q**. Cut two body pieces and two arm pieces from red aida cloth. Cut two head pieces from pink aida cloth, and four boot pieces from black cotton fabric.

2. Cross-stitch the facial features on one head piece, using black for the eyes, pink for the nose and cheek spots, and red for the mouth. Cross-stitch the apron front and buttons on one body piece, using white floss. Cross-stitch white apron sashes on the other body piece, and a white cuff on each arm piece.

3. Stitch, turn, stuff, and assemble Mrs. Santa's body, head, arms, and boots as described for the Snowman. (See "Making the body," steps 3 through 7 for the Snowman.) On step 6, turn the arm edges to the inside on the diagonal, as described for Santa's arms. Wrap an 8-inch length of white satin ribbon around Mrs. Santa's stitched neck seam, and tie it in a bow at the front.

Figure Q

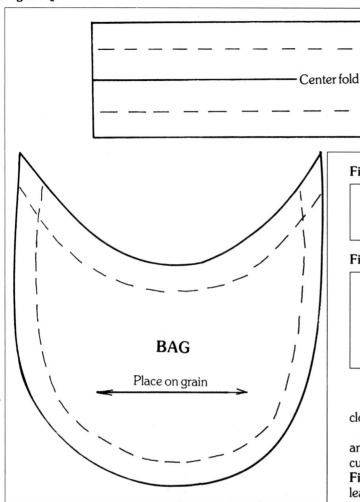

Center fold

BAG

Place on grain

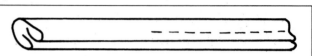

Figure R

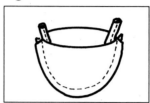

Figure S

Figure T

Making the hair, hat, and bag

1. Mrs. Santa's hair is made like Santa. (See steps 3, 4, and 5 under "Adding the hat, hair, and bag" in the instructions for Santa.) Give Mrs. Santa white curls all over her head, except for the face of course.

2. Cut a small holly leaf from green felt, and add a red felt holly berry (or a red-headed pin). Attach these to Mrs. Santa's hair at one side of the forehead.

3. To make the hat, run a line of gathering stitches close to one long edge of the 1 x 5-inch hat fabric. Press a narrow hem allowance to the wrong side along the opposite long edge. Place the two short edges right sides together and stitch the seam. Pull up the gathers and secure the threads to form the center of the hat. Glue or whipstitch the cap to the top of Mrs. Santa's head, over the curls. Glue the red pompon to the center of the hat.

4. Glue or whipstitch the white eyelet around the bottom of the body, overlapping the ends at the back.

5. To make the goodie bag, use the full-size patterns to cut two bag pieces from ivory aida cloth and two additional bag pieces from the lining fabric you have chosen. Cut one strap piece from aida cloth.

6. Cross-stitch the word "goodies" in the center of one aida cloth bag piece, using green floss.

7. Place the two aida cloth bag pieces right sides together and stitch close to the long curved edge, leaving the upper curved edge open and unstitched (as on the Snowman's bag, **Figure H**). Stitch the two lining bags right sides together, leaving the upper edge unstitched and leaving a 1½-inch opening at the bottom of the seam (as you did on the Snowman's bag, **Figure I**). Turn the stitched lining right side out, but leave the stitched outer bag with right sides together.

8. Press a ¼-inch allowance to the wrong side on each long edge of the strap piece. Fold the piece in half lengthwise, wrong sides together (**Figure R**), and stitch. Place the stitched strap inside the outer bag, along the curve, allowing the ends to extend above the corners of the bag (**Figure S**).

9. Now place the lining inside the bag (**Figure T**), being careful not to disturb the strap. With upper raw edges even, stitch the lining to the bag around the upper edge, catching the ends of the strap in the seam. Clip the curves. Turn the bag and lining right side out through the opening in the bottom of the lining. Whipstitch the opening together, tuck the lining inside the turned bag, and pull the strap up. Press.

10. Insert Mrs. Santa's arm through the strap, fold her arm forward so that the strap is between her arm and body, and glue or whipstitch the strap and arm in place.

11. Cut a small holly leaf from green felt and add a red felt holly berry (or red-headed pin). Glue them to the bag.

12. To form the hanging loop, fold the remaining 12-inch length of white satin ribbon in half, and knot the ends. Stitch the knotted ends to Mrs. Santa's back, just below the head. Tack the loop to Mrs. Santa's head just below her cap, so that she will hang plumb.

Santa Claus Display Box

Use this jolly bit of decor to hold and display Christmas cards or candy. It's a very easy project to make.

Materials

One heavy cardboard box, 5½ x 10¼ inches, and 4¾ inches high. The box need not have a top.

One flat piece of cardboard, 5¼ x 10 inches.

6 x 34-inch piece of red 14-count aida cloth.

12-inch square of ivory-colored 14-count aida cloth.

½ yard of red-and-white pin-dot fabric.

1 yard of green satin ribbon, 1½ inches wide.

Embroidery floss in black, red, and white.

Tapestry and regular needles, pins, red and white thread, half a bag of polyester fiberfill, glue gun and hot-melt adhesive (or substitute white glue), sewing machine, steam iron, pattern paper.

Cross-stitch

1. A color-coded cross-stitch graph for Santa's face is provided in **Figure A**. (The dotted outline will be enlarged and used as a cutting pattern later, so disregard the line and the two placement circles near the lower edge at this time.) Stitch the design in the center of the white aida cloth, and then press gently on the wrong side using a steam setting.

2. A graph for Santa's hands is provided in **Figure B**. Stitch the hands in the center of the red aida cloth rectangle, using white floss. Press.

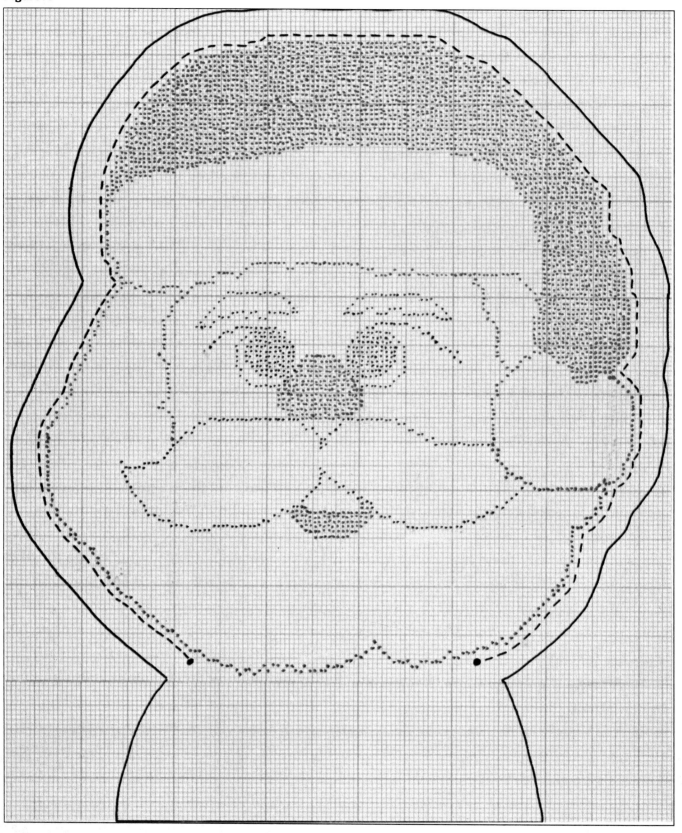

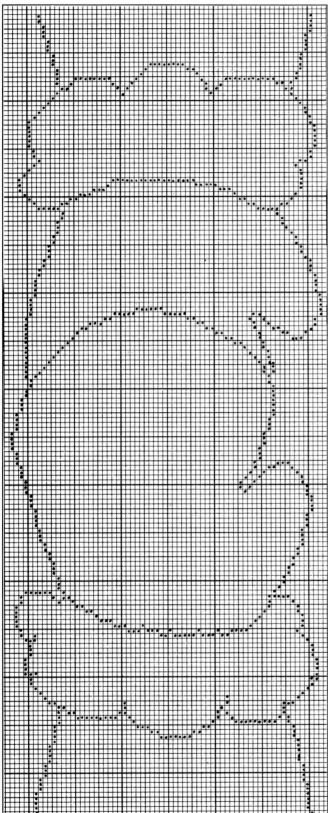

Figure C

Making the head

1. Trace the full-size head outline in **Figure A**, to make a paper pattern.

2. Center the head pattern over the cross-stitched face, and cut the cloth to the shape of the pattern. Cut an additional head from red pin-dot fabric.

3. Pin the aida and pin-dot heads right sides together and stitch the seam around the long contoured edge. Leave the straight neck edge and the lower sides below the small circles open and unstitched (**Figure C**).

4. Clip the curves and turn the head right side out. Press gently. Press the remaining raw edges to the inside along the seam lines. Stuff the head firmly with fiberfill, leaving the lower portion below the circles unstuffed.

Covering the box

The cardboard box is completely covered with fabric; with red aida cloth on the outer sides, and with pin-dot fabric on the bottom and inner sides. The covering and lining are sewn together to form a fabric box, and slipped over the cardboard box. A fabric-covered piece of cardboard makes a lining for the bottom of the box.

1. Cut a 6 x 34-inch piece of red pin-dot fabric for the side lining. Pin the side lining and the cross-stitched red aida cloth right sides together, and stitch the seam along one long raw edge. Press the seam open.

Figure D

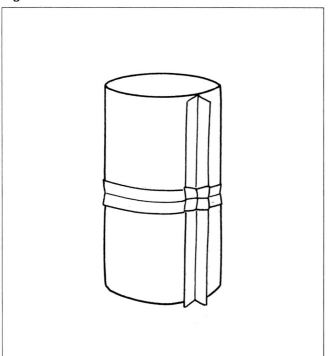

Figure E

Figure F

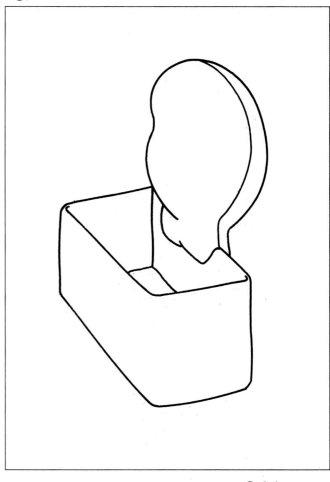

2. Fold the lining and aida assembly in half widthwise, placing right sides together, and stitch the center back seam (**Figure E**). Press the seam open.

3. Cut a 6 ¾ x 11¾-inch piece of pin-dot fabric for the bottom cover. Pin the bottom cover to the red aida cloth cover, placing right sides together (**Figure E**). Be very careful to place the pieces correctly, so that the center of the cross-stitched hands design is in line with the center of one long edge of the bottom cover. Stitch the seams carefully, easing the fabric at the corners. Clip the corners and turn the entire assembly right side out.

4. Slip the cardboard box inside the cover and lining assembly, and fold the pin-dot lining to the inside. Glue the raw edges of the lining inside the bottom of the box.

5. Cut a 7½ x 12-inch piece of pin-dot fabric for the inner lining. Place the inner lining wrong side up on a flat surface, and center the flat piece of cardboard on top. Fold the edges of the fabric around the edges of the cardboard, and glue them to the top.

6. Turn the fabric-covered inner lining piece right side up, and insert it into the box. Push it down to the bottom so that it covers the raw edges of the box lining fabric.

Finishing touches

1. Center Santa's head over the back long edge of the box, so that the open lower edges of the head straddle the side of the box (**Figure G**). Glue or whipstitch the head to the cover and lining fabrics.

2. Wrap the green and white ribbon around Santa's neck, and tie a bow at the front. At the center back, tack the ribbon to the red cover fabric to stabilize the head.

Kissing Ball

Here's a festive way to hang mistletoe for the holiday season, and collect extra kisses in the bargain!

Materials

7 x 33-inch piece of white 14-count aida cloth.

¼ yard of light-weight white cotton fabric.

4 yards of 1-inch-wide white lace trim.

4 yards of green-and-red-plaid corded piping.

2 yards of green-and-red-plaid fabric-covered cording to match the piping. If you can't find piping and cording to match, purchase them in coordinating colors. As an alternative, you can purchase fabric and plain cotton cord, and make your own piping and cording.

2 yards of 1½-inch-wide red-and-green-striped felt ribbon.

Four glittery white bells, each approximately 1 inch tall. (These are usually sold as cake decorations.)

A sprig of mistletoe, live or artificial.

Embroidery floss in green and red.

Tapestry and regular needles, pins, scissors, sewing machine, white and red thread.

Cross-stitch

You'll find cross-stitch graphs for the Christmas tree and NOEL in **Figure A**. Cut the aida cloth into two strips, each 3½ x 33 inches. Stitch a repeating tree motif along the center of one strip, using green floss. Allow approximately 3½ inches of space at each end of the strip, and reverse the direction of the trees when you reach the middle of the strip, so that they will all appear right side up when the strip is curved into a circular shape.

Work a repeating NOEL design along the center of the other strip, using red floss. Allow 3½ inches of space at each end of the strip, and reverse the direction of the words when you reach the middle of the strip. Press both strips on the wrong side.

Trimming the strips

Note: All seam allowances are ½ inch.

1. Place one aida cloth strip right side up on a flat surface. Pin a length of piping to one long edge of the strip, around the short end, and back along the remaining long edge (**Figure B**). Place the raw edges of the piping even with the edges of the aida cloth, so that the corded edge extends in toward the center. Baste the piping in place.

2. Pin a length of lace trim over the piping, placing the straight edge of the lace ¼ inch from the raw edges of the piping and aida cloth. The scalloped edge of the lace should extend inward. Allow a generous amount of lace at the corners, so it won't be stretched flat when it is turned outward. Baste the lace in place.

Figure B

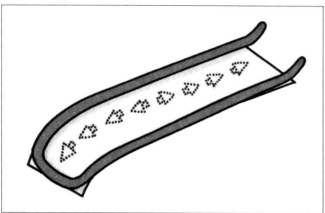

Figure C

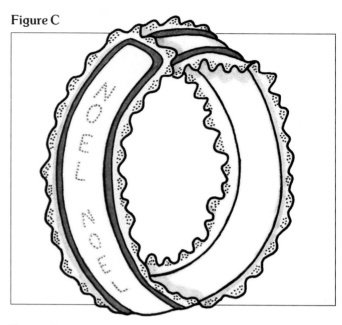

Figure D

3. Cut a 3½ x 33-inch piece of white cotton fabric to serve as a lining. Pin the fabric strip right side down over the aida cloth. (The piping and lace will be sandwiched between.) Stitch the seams along both long edges and the trimmed short edge, through all thicknesses. Clip the corners and turn the strip right side out. Press the seam allowances to the inside on the remaining raw edges, and whipstitch the open edges together.

4. Repeat steps 1 through 3, using the remaining cross-stitched aida cloth strip.

Assembling the ball

1. Bend one of the trimmed strips into a circle, placing the cross-stitching on the outside. Overlap the ends by approximately 2 inches, and tack them together (**Figure C**).

2. Fold and tack the remaining strip as you did the first one, placing it at right angles around the first strip as shown in **Figure D**.

3. Cut a 12-inch length of fabric-covered cording and tie a knot at each end. Tack one end under the crossed strips at the top of the ball, and the other end over the strips at the bottom (**Figure D**). This will help hold the shape.

4. Cut four lengths of cording: one 16 inches, one 14 inches, and two 12 inches. Knot the upper ends of the cords together (**Figure E**). Tie the free end of each cord in a bow, tie a knot at the very end, and tack a bell to each bow. Tack the large knot the crossed strips inside the top of the ball.

5. Cut the felt ribbon in half, and loop each piece several times to form a fancy bow, tacked together at the center. Tack one bow under the crossed strips at the bottom of the ball, and the remaining bow over the crossed strips at the top of the ball.

6. To form a hanging loop, cut a 9-inch length of cording and fold it in half. Tie the ends together and tack the loop over the bow at the top of the ball. Tie the remaining length of cording in a bow around the stem of the mistletoe, and tack it to the bow at the bottom of the kissing ball.

7. Hang your creation in a prominent place, and pucker!

Figure E

Celebrations

Ewe's
My Valentine

This frilly, silly valentine can be presented on top of a heart-shaped box of candy, or by itself as a wall hanging since the back is finished too. The cross-stitched message is short and sweet, so you can complete the entire project in just a few hours.

Materials

12-inch square of red 14-count aida cloth.
⅝ yard of white satin ribbon, 1 inch wide.
6-inch length of pink satin ribbon, ⅛ inch wide.
2 yards of white organdy trim, 2 inches wide.
¾ yard of light-weight white fabric with a small red print.
1 yard of white corded piping, ⅛ inch in diameter.
One small skein of off-white crewel yarn.
Two small scraps of black felt.
Embroidery floss in black and white.
Two 10-inch squares of medium-weight cardboard.
Small quantity of polyester fiberfill.
Glue gun and hot-melt adhesive, or substitute white glue and several clothespins or clamps to secure your work while the glue dries.
Tapestry and regular needles, pins, scissors, sewing machine, pattern paper, white thread, steam iron.

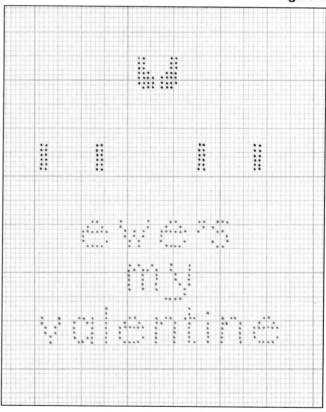

Cross-stitch

A cross-stitch graph is provided in **Figure A**. (The strange-looking designs above the valentine message are the legs and faces of the two sheep.) Stitch the message, centering it between the sides of the aida cloth square and placing the word "valentine" approximately 3 inches from the lower edge of the cloth. Count spaces to determine the placement of the remaining stitches. We worked the message in white and the sheeps' legs and faces in black. Press gently.

Figure B

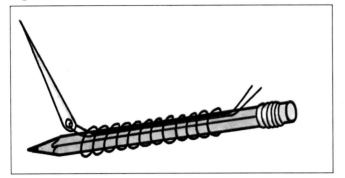

Figure C

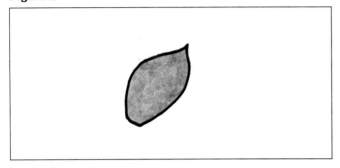

Finishing the design

1. The sheep's bodies are made of yarn curls. To make the curls, you'll be working with the following supplies and tools: a continuous length of crewel yarn, a needle threaded with heavy-duty thread, and a pencil or other thin roundish object. Begin by stitching one end of the yarn to the aida cloth, above the cross-stitched legs of one sheep.

2. Wrap the yarn around the pencil approximately fifteen times. Insert the needle between the yarn and pencil, and push it out through the opposite end (**Figure B**). Remove the pencil, compressing the curl, and take another stitch into the aida cloth to secure the curl.

3. Continue making curls in this manner until you have completed a body and head for each sheep. The exact shapes of the bodies are not important, but try to make the left-hand sheep a bit smaller because this will be the ewe. (When the sheep are completed you can spread, flatten, stretch, and otherwise rearrange the yarn loops so that the overall shapes look right, and then take a few stitches with the needle and thread to secure the loops in place.) Stitch the yarn end to the aida cloth underneath the final curl on each sheep.

4. A full-size ear pattern is provided in **Figure C**. Trace the pattern and cut one ear from the black felt. Fold the ear in half lengthwise, and glue it together just at the short straight end. Glue this end to the yarn curls of the right-hand sheep. Cut and attach a slightly smaller ear for the ewe.

5. Wrap the pink ribbon around the ewe's neck, and tie it in a bow on top.

Assembling the front

1. A scale drawing for the heart is provided in **Figure D**. Enlarge the drawing to a full-size paper pattern.

Figure D   1 square = 1 inch

HEART

Figure E

2. Place the pattern on the cross-stitched aida cloth so that the sheep are in the center, and cut the cloth to the shape of the pattern.

3. Pin the piping around the aida cloth heart on the right side of the fabric, overlapping the ends at the top center (**Figure E**). The raw edges of the piping should lie along the raw edge of the aida cloth, and the corded edge of the piping should extend in toward the center. Stitch as close to the cording as possible, using a zipper foot attachment on your machine. Clip the curves.

4. Cut a heart-shaped piece of cardboard, making it ¾ inch smaller than the heart-shaped pattern all the way around. Place the cardboard heart on a flat surface and glue fiberfill to it on one side only, about 1½ inches deep.

5. Center the cross-stitched aida cloth over the fiberfill and cardboard, and turn the entire assembly upside down so that the aida cloth rests flat on the work surface. Glue the clipped edges of the cloth to the back of the cardboard, so that the corded edge of the piping forms a border around the edge of the heart. Before glueing the last few inches of the aida cloth edge, you may wish to add or remove some fiberfill. Glue the piping ends to the cardboard so that they do not show on the front.

6. Tie the length of satin ribbon in a bow, and tack or glue it to the front of the aida cloth heart at the top center.

Adding the ruffles and back

1. To make the white inner ruffle, run a line of basting stitches ¼ inch from the bound edge of the organdy trim. Pull the threads to gather the trim until it measures 33 inches long. Adjust the gathers evenly, and run a line of regular stitches over the basting stitches to secure the gathers.

2. Glue the gathered edge of the organdy to the back of the aida-covered cardboard heart, overlapping the ends at the top center. The trim should extend about 1½ inches beyond the finished edge of the heart (**Figure F**).

3. To make the patterned outer ruffle, cut two 7 x 36-inch strips of white patterned fabric and piece them together to form one continuous strip, 7 x 71 inches. Press the center seam open, and press a ½-inch allowance to the wrong side on each short end. Fold the strip in half lengthwise, placing wrong sides together, and press. Run a line of basting stitches ¼ inch from the long raw edges, and pull the threads to gather the strip to a length of 33 inches, as you did the organdy. Adjust the gathers evenly, then and run a line of regular stitches over the basting stitches to secure the gathers.

4. Glue the gathered edge of this ruffle to the back of the cardboard heart (over the organdy), overlapping the ends at the top center. The folded edge of the ruffle should extend approximately 3 inches beyond the cardboard.

5. Cut a second cardboard heart, this time to the exact size of the pattern. Cut an additional heart from the white patterned fabric, making it 1 inch larger than the pattern all the way around.

6. Place the fabric heart wrong side up on a flat surface, and center the cardboard heart on top. Clip the fabric up to the cardboard all the way around. Fold the fabric edges over the edge of the cardboard and glue them in place.

7. Glue the two heart-shaped assemblies wrong sides together. You may wish to add a hanging loop.

Christmas Candle Skirt

Dress up a red or green Christmas candle for a lovely addition to your holiday decorations.

Materials

10 x 36-inch piece of red cotton fabric with white pin dots.
6 x 36-inch piece of green 14-count aida cloth.
1 yard of ¾-inch-wide bias binding.
1 yard of ½-inch-wide white decorative trim. We used trim made of overlapping braid loops.
1 yard of ¼-inch-wide green ribbon.
One 3-inch-diameter red or green candle, 9 inches tall.
Embroidery floss in white, pink, red, and beige.
Tapestry and regular needles, pins, scissors, sewing machine, steam iron.

Cross-stitch

We stitched holly leaves and berries in a repeating design along the entire strip of aida cloth. A graph for the design is provided in **Figure A**. Work the design so that it does not come closer than 1 inch to any edge of the cloth. Make each leaf half white and half beige. In each cluster of berries, make two berries half red and half pink. Make the remaining berry half beige and half white.

Assembling the skirt

Note: All seam allowances are ½ inch.

1. Fold the cross-stitched aida cloth in half widthwise, placing right sides together, and stitch the seam along the two short edges (**Figure B**). Press the seam open and turn the aida cloth right side out.

2. Follow the same procedures to stitch and press the red pin-dot fabric. Leave this tube inside out.

3. Slip the aida cloth tube inside the pin-dot tube, with upper edges even, matching seams. Stitch the seam around the upper edges (**Figure C**).

Figure B

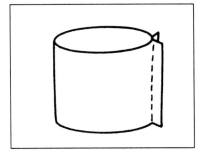

Figure C

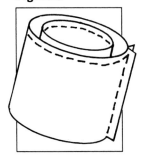

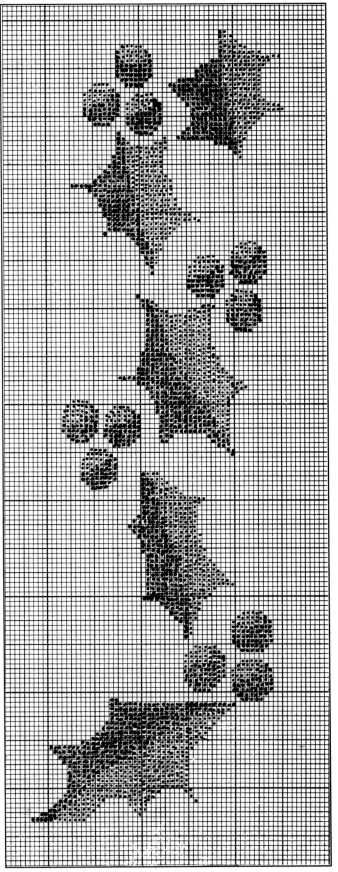

Figure D

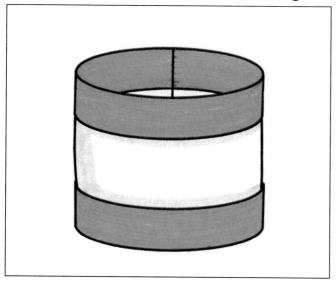

Figure E

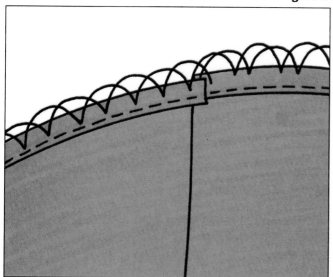

Figure F

Figure G

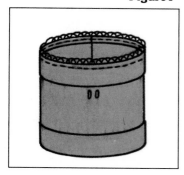

4. Slide the red fabric upward until the lower edge is even with the lower edge of the aida cloth. (Be sure that it does not twist sideways – the vertical seams should still match.) Stitch the seam around the lower edges, as you did the upper seam, but leave a 3-inch opening in the lower seam.

5. Press all upper and lower seam allowances toward the aida cloth. Turn the assembly right side out through the opening and whipstitch the opening edges together. Adjust the fabrics so that the aida cloth is on the outside, with a 1-inch border of red fabric showing at the top and bottom (**Figure D**), and press.

Adding the ribbon and trim

1. Stitch the decorative white trim to the upper edge of the tube, placing the bound edge of the trim on the inside just below the folded edge (**Figure E**). The ends of the trim should overlap slightly at the vertical seam on the tube.

2. Temporarily flatten the tube, to find the point exactly opposite the vertical seam. Work two vertical buttonholes, one on each side of this point, just below the upper edge of the aida cloth (**Figure F**). The buttonholes should be about ½ inch long, worked through all thicknesses of fabric.

3. Turn the tube inside out, so that the red pin dot fabric is on the outside. Pin the bias binding around the tube, beginning and ending at the buttonholes (**Figure G**) and turning the raw ends of the binding under. Stitch close to each long edge of the binding. This will serve as a casing for the ribbon.

4. To thread the ribbon through the casing, attach a safety pin to one end of the ribbon and insert the pin between the binding and red fabric at one end of the binding. Work the safety pin along through the casing, and out at the opposite end. Pull the ribbon until the ends are of equal length.

5. Thread one ribbon end through one of the buttonholes, and pull it through to the aida cloth side. Thread the remaining ribbon end through the other buttonhole. Tie a knot at each end of the ribbon, to keep them from slipping back inside the casing.

6. Turn the skirt right side out again, and insert the candle inside. Pull up the ribbon ends to gather the skirt around the candle. Tie the ribbon in a bow.

Changeable Bermuda Bag

The beauty of this handbag is its versatility. It has an inner lining that is permanently attached to the handles, and a lined outer cover that is buttoned in place. You can stitch up an outer cover to match every outfit you have, and change the cover without having to dump out the contents of your purse – ever!

Materials

½ yard of white cotton broadcloth.

½ yard of fabric for the back and gussets of the cover – we used red calico.

9 x 11½-inch piece of 22-count hardanger cloth to coordinate with the cover fabric.

Embroidery floss in the color (or colors) of your choice. We used red only, but you could use 2 contrasting colors.

1½ yards of cotton cord, ¼ inch or smaller in diameter. You'll be using this with cover fabric to make matching corded piping. If you prefer, purchase corded piping in a coordinating color.

Eight matching buttons, about ½ inch in diameter.

Bermuda bag handles, 9½ inches wide and 6 inches tall. (You can purchase bermuda-bag handles at most craft or large fabric stores. Many stores carry handles with an inner lining already attached, which means you won't have to make an inner lining. If you already own a bermuda bag, you can alter the dimensions of our patterns to fit your bag.)

Figure A

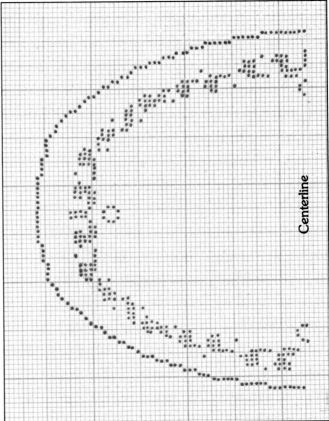

Centerline

Embroidery hoop, tapestry needle, sewing machine, scissors, pins, measuring tape, pattern paper, sewing needle, and thread to match the fabrics.

Optional materials

You'll need some additional supplies if you're a glutton for doing it yourself, and wish to make the wooden handles. To make the handles, you'll need:

10 x 14-inch piece of ⅜-inch-thick veneer-core plywood. We used baltic birch, but any high quality veneer-core plywood will do. (We have used solid wood, but once used some that was improperly seasoned and wound up with a very strangely warped set of handles. So plywood is a better bet.)

Two metal hinges, about 1 inch long, with ¼-inch-wide flanges and screws to fit.

Sandpaper, wood stain, polyurethane varnish, wood glue, and a small paint brush.

To cut and attach the handles, you'll need a saber saw or coping saw, electric or hand drill with ½-inch-diameter bit, screwdriver, staple gun, and a few staples with ⅜-inch legs. If you don't have a staple gun, substitute small tacks and a hammer.

To Wear & Carry

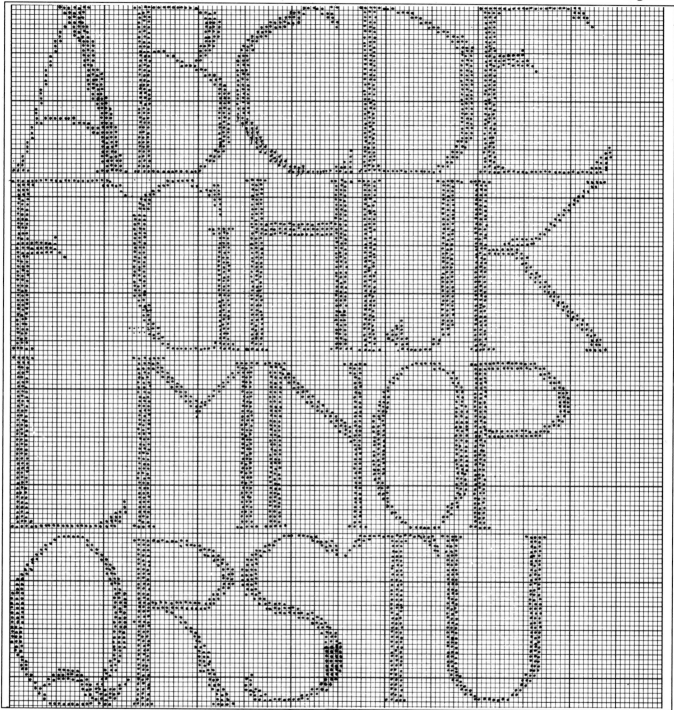

Cross-stitch

You'll find cross-stitch graphs for this project in **Figure A**. There are two alphabet graphs (one large and one small), and a graph for one-half of the border design (the other half is a mirror image). The larger alphabet is used for the last name initial, which is worked in the center of the monogram.

The smaller alphabet is used for the first and middle initials, which are worked on either side.

Cross-stitch the border on the hardanger cloth. Create your monogram by stitching the appropriate letters inside the border.

To Wear & Carry

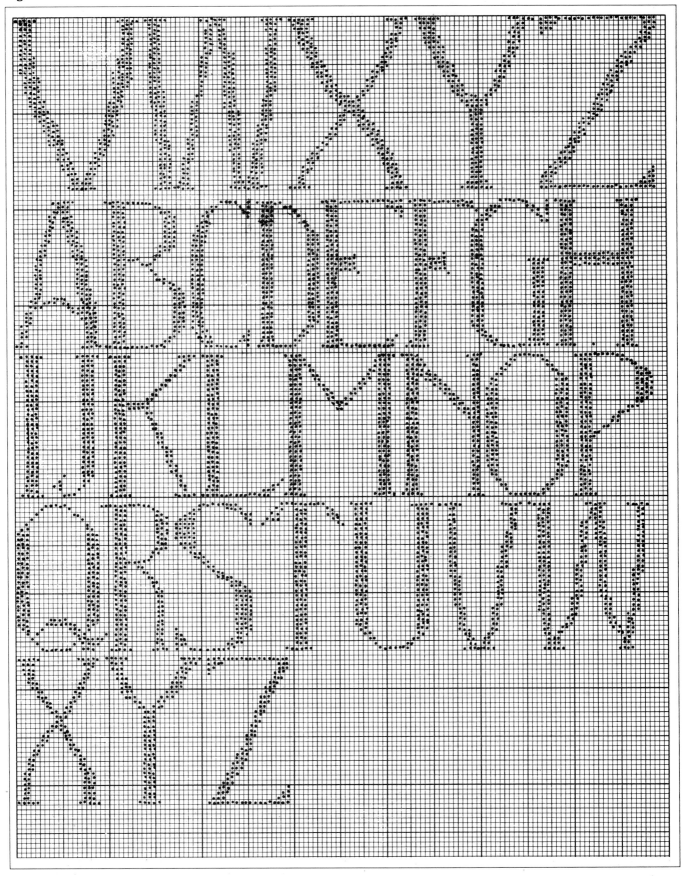

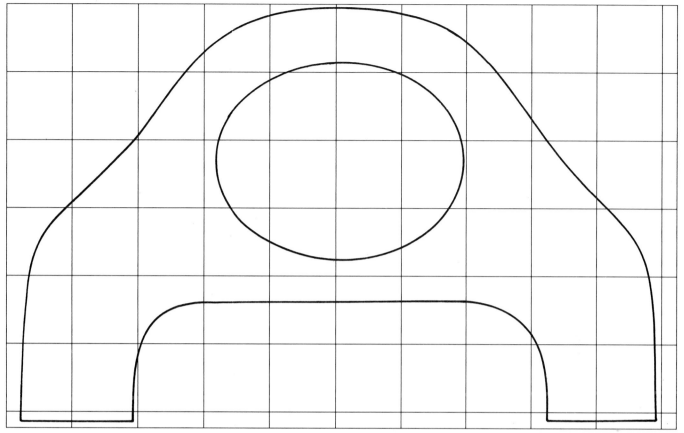

Figure C

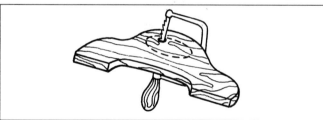

Figure D

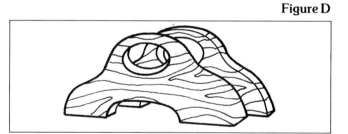

Figure E

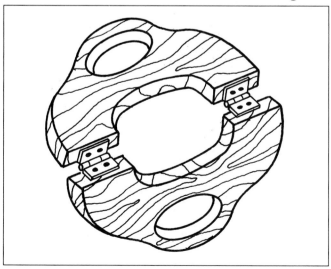

Making the handle assembly

1. A scale drawing of the handle is given in **Figure B**. Enlarge the drawing to a full-size paper pattern, and transfer the outline of the oval cutout to the pattern.

2. Cut one handle from plywood, and use this piece as a pattern to cut an identical handle. To make the oval cutout, first transfer the outline from the pattern to each wooden piece. Drill a hole just inside the cutting line, insert the saw blade through the hole, and cut around the outline (**Figure C**).

3. Place the handles together, face to face, choosing the best-looking sides to face outward. Sand both handles, rounding off all of the outer edges as shown in **Figure D**. Do not round off the edges on the inner sides. Don't forget to round the outer edges of the oval cutouts.

4. Stain and varnish the handles and allow them sufficient time to dry. Hinge them together at the lower edges (**Figure E**), using glue and screws.

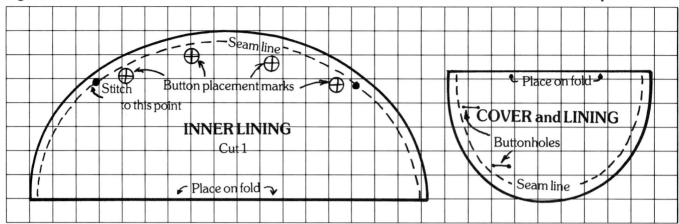

Making the inner lining

Note: All seam allowances are ½ inch unless otherwise specified in the instructions.

1. Scale drawings for the sewing patterns are provided in **Figure F**. Enlarge the drawings to full-size paper patterns.

2. Cut one inner lining piece from broadcloth, paying attention to the "place on fold" notation. Transfer the large dots and the button placement marks to the fabric.

3. With the inner lining piece still folded in half right sides together, stitch the two side seams (between the fold and the dot on each side). Clip the seam allowances up to the seam line at each dot. Press gently with a steam iron, turning the seam allowances of the remaining raw edges to the right side as you press. Topstitch the turned seam allowances.

4. Attach four buttons along each curved upper edge of the inner lining on the wrong side of the fabric. (Refer to the button placement marks on the pattern.)

5. Use staples or small tacks to attach the inner lining to the outer sides of the handles, about ¾ inch from the lower edges **(Figure G)**. Be sure to use plenty of staples or tacks, especially if you carry lots of life's necessities in your purse.

Preparing the cover and lining pieces

1. Use the full-size cover pattern to cut one back cover piece from calico (or your chosen fabric), and two lining pieces from broadcloth. In addition, center the pattern over the cross-stitched design on the hardanger cloth, and cut the cloth to the shape of the pattern. This will be the front cover. (Staystitch the edges of the hardanger cloth to keep them from fraying.) Transfer the buttonhole placement dots to the front and back covers.

2. A gusset joins the front and back covers, and another joins the front and back linings. Cut two gussets, each 2¼ x 21½ inches, one from calico and one from broadcloth. Turn a ½-inch seam allowance to the wrong side on both short ends of each gusset, and press.

3. If you did not purchase corded piping, now's the time

Figure G

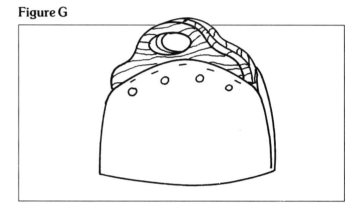

Figure H

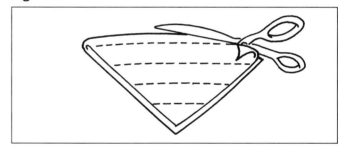

to make some. Cut the remaining calico into 2-inch-wide bias strips. (The easiest way to find the true bias is to fold a square of fabric into a triangle, being sure the edges of the square are cut along the straight grain of the fabric. Then simply cut along the fold, as shown in **Figure H**). Piece two or more strips together at the ends to form two continuous strips, each 2 feet long. (When joining bias strips, always stitch along the straight grain of the fabric as shown in **Figure I**. It looks strange when you're stitching, but it works!)

4. To assemble the corded piping, place one bias strip on a flat surface wrong side up. Place a 2-foot length of cotton cord along the center of the strip, and fold the raw edges of the fabric together, encasing the cord. Use a zipper foot attachment to stitch through both layers of fabric, as close to the cord as possible. Repeat this procedure using the remaining bias strip and length of cord.

Figure I

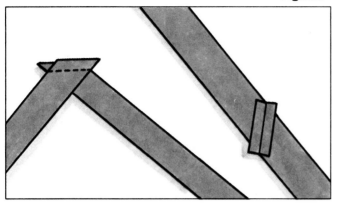

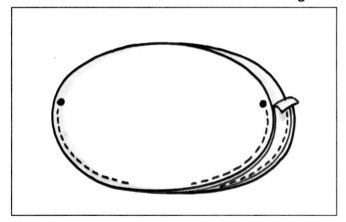

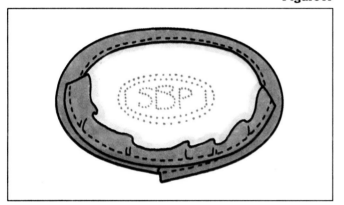

Figure L

Assembling the cover and lining

1. Begin by assembling the cover. Pin one length of piping to the right side of the front cover, starting and ending at the bottom center **(Figure J)**. The line of stitching on the piping should be placed along the seam line of the cover, with the corded edge extending inward and the raw edges pointing outward. Overlap the ends at the bottom of the cover. Machine or hand baste the piping in place.

2. Pin the calico gusset to the bottom of the front cover between the large dots **(Figure K)**, placing right sides together. (The piping will be sandwiched between the gusset and cover.) Stitch along the seam line all the way around the cover.

3. Repeat step 1 using the calico back cover and the remaining length of piping.

4. Repeat step 2 to attach the remaining free long edge of the calico gusset to the back cover between the large dots (right sides together, raw edges even). Press all seams gently and turn the assembled cover right side out.

5. Now assemble the lining in the same manner (but without any piping), using the broadcloth front and back linings and gusset. When you are stitching the gusset to the back lining, leave a 4-inch-long opening at the bottom center **(Figure L)**. Press the seams, and leave the lining inside out.

6. Slip the assembled cover inside the lining, so that the raw upper edges are even. Stitch the back cover and lining together along the upper edge between the large dots (where the gussets end). Stitch the front cover and lining together in the same manner. Turn the entire assembly right side out by stuffing it through the opening at the bottom of the back lining/cover seam, and then whipstitch the opening together. Gently push the lining down inside the outer cover. Whipstitch the turned edges of the gusset and gusset lining together at each side of the bag.

7. Work one buttonhole between each set of small placement dots on the front and back of the cover. Check the placement to make sure the buttonholes correspond to the buttons already attached to the inner lining. Slip the finished outer cover over the inner lining and button it in place.

The Face Case

The whimsical design of this glasses case makes it a terrific gift item. It's a great bazaar idea too, since the cross-stitching and sewing are a snap!

Materials

8½ x 13-inch piece of white 11-count aida cloth.
8½ x 13-inch piece of deep blue cotton velvet.
1⅛ yards of white braided piping.
A pair of white frog closures.
The panty portion from a pair of white pantyhose.
Embroidery floss in blue, green, black, red, and pink.
Small quantity of polyester fiberfill.
Heavy-duty and regular white threads, tapestry and regular needles, pins, steam iron, scissors, sewing machine with a zipper foot attachment, and measuring tape.

Cross-stitch

You'll find a color-coded cross-stitch graph for the eyes and mouth in **Figure A**. Stitch the design on the aida cloth so that the features are centered between the side edges. The bottom of the mouth should be 4 inches from the lower edge of the cloth, and the tops of the eyes should be 5¼ inches from the upper edge.

Figure A

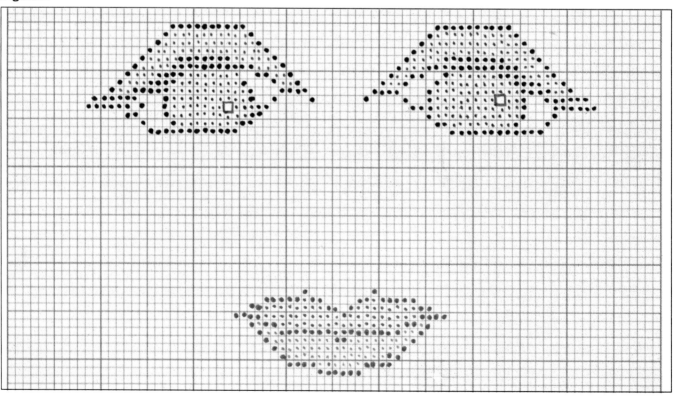

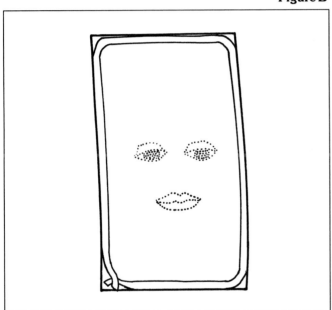

Figure C

Assembling the case

1. Pin the braided piping around the edge of the aida cloth, on the right side of the fabric, as shown in **Figure B**. (The rounded braided edge of the piping should point toward the center, and should lie about ⅝ inch from the raw edge of the aida cloth. The raw edges of the piping should point outward.) You'll be rounding the corners when you stitch, so don't try to make the piping conform to the square angles at the corners – just pin it around them in nice, easy curves. Begin and end at a lower corner as shown, overlapping the ends of the piping. Baste the piping in place.

2. Pin the velvet right side down over the aida cloth (the piping will be sandwiched between). Use a zipper foot attachment on your machine and stitch the seam around all four edges, as close as possible to the round piping braid. Follow the rounded contours at the corners, and leave a 3-inch opening along the lower edge.

3. Trim and clip the seam allowances at the corners. Turn the case right side out, press gently, and whipstitch the opening edges together.

Adding the nose

1. A nose made of stuffed, soft sculptured pantyhose will hold your glasses in place. Cut a 4-inch-diameter circle of white pantyhose, using the heavier panty portion of the hose. Wrap the circle of hose around a 3-inch-diameter ball of fiberfill, gather the raw edge tightly together, and tie it off with a length of heavy-duty thread (**Figure C**).

2. Soft sculpturing is something of an inexact art, since the shapes that result depend on several variables: how tightly you pull the thread, the exact placement of entry and exit points, how tightly the hose is stuffed, etc.

The approximate entry and exit points used to sculpture the nose are illustrated in **Figure D**. Follow the instructions below, experimenting with thread tension and exact entry and exit placement, until you have created an object that resembles a nose (however slightly). Use a single strand of heavy-duty thread, and just pull out what you've done if it doesn't look right. Remember that you can squish, prod, and kneed the stuffed ball as much as necessary to make it behave.

The illustration shows the stuffed ball from the top. If you could see through it, you would see the tied portion on the bottom, which will ultimately be sewn flat against the aida cloth face. For your reading enjoyment, the "tied portion" will henceforth be called the "knot."

a. Enter at the knot and exit at 1. Reenter at 1 (not the exact point from which you just exited, but right next to it), push the needle straight through the stuffing, and exit at 2.

b. Pull the thread down around the outside of the stuffed ball, enter at one side of the knot, and push the needle through the knot to exit on the opposite side. Pull the thread until a ridge forms between points 1 and 2.

c. Reenter at the knot and exit at 3. Reenter at 3, push the needle straight through the nose, and exit at 4.

d. Pull the thread down around the outside, and enter at the knot. Exit on the opposite side of the knot and pull the thread until the ridge between points 1 and 2 extends itself down to points 3 and 4. Take an additional stitch through the knot to secure the ridge. This is the bridge of the nose.

e. Continue to work with the same needle and thread to form the nostrils, following the entry and exit points illustrated in **Figure E**. Enter at the knot and exit at 5. Reenter at 5, push the needle down through the stuffing, and exit at 6.

f. Pull the thread across the surface, enter at 7 and exit at 8. Pull the thread until the end of the nose forms between points 6 and 7.

g. Hold the thread taut as you pull it across the surface, enter at 6 and exit at 5. Pull the thread across the surface, enter at 7 and exit at 6.

h. Pull the thread around the outside, down to the knot. Enter at the knot and exit at 7. Pull the thread across the surface, down to the knot again. Enter at the knot, lock the stitch and cut the thread.

3. Whipstitch the sculptured nose to the aida cloth, in the center of the cross-stitched facial features. Be careful not to stitch through the velvet.

Finishing

Place a pair of eyeglasses face down over the cross-stitched eyes, so that the nosepiece rests securely on the stuffed nose. Fold the bottom of the case up, fold the top down, and mark the positions where the frog closures should be attached (**Figure F**). Handstitch the frogs in place.

Figure D

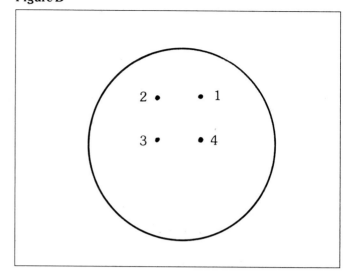

Figure E

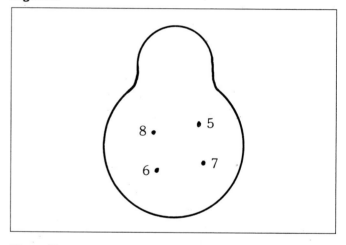

Figure F

Baby Bonnet

Make a frilly eyelet bonnet with pastel cross-stitched hearts for your favorite very young lady.

Materials

11 x 36-inch piece of white eyelet fabric.
2³⁄₈ yards of 1-inch-wide white eyelet trim.
15-inch length of pre-gathered 4-inch-wide white eyelet trim. Or purchase a 30-inch length of ungathered trim and gather it yourself.
1 yard of ¾-inch-wide white ribbon eyelet.
2¼ yards of 1-inch-wide white satin ribbon.
1³⁄₈ yards of 1-inch-wide double-fold seam binding.
2¾ x 15-inch piece of 11-count aida cloth.
6-inch length of ½-inch-wide elastic.
Embroidery floss in pink, lilac, blue, and green.

Cross-stitch

We suggest that you check to make sure the bonnet will fit before you work on the cross-stitch. First, measure the baby's head from one ear lobe to the other, over the top of the head. If the measurement is less than 12 inches, cut the aida cloth strip 1 inch longer than your measurement. Use the shortened strip as a guide when cutting the lengths of eyelet that are attached to it (steps 1 through 3 under "Assembling the front" section), and when gathering the front edge of the eyelet fabric (step 4).

You'll find a color-coded cross-stitch graph for the bordered heart design in **Figure A**. Work the design in the center of the aida cloth strip, and staystitch ¼ inch from all edges.

To Wear & Carry

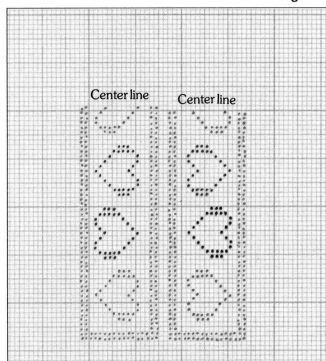

Center line   Center line

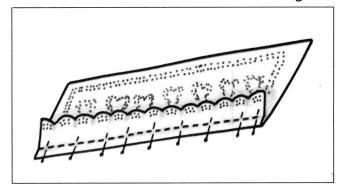

Assembling the front

Note: All seam allowances are ½ inch unless otherwise specified.

1. Cut a 15-inch length of narrow eyelet trim. Pin it to the aida cloth, placing right sides together, so that the bound edge of the eyelet is ¼ inch from one long raw edge of the aida cloth (**Figure B**). The scalloped edge of the eyelet should extend in toward the center of the strip. Baste along the stitching line.

2. Pin the pre-gathered eyelet trim over the narrow eyelet and aida cloth, following the procedures described in step 1. Stitch along the seam line, through all thicknesses. Turn the eyelet trims outward, and press the seam allowances toward the aida cloth. This will be the front of the bonnet.

3. Repeat step 1 to baste another 15-inch length of narrow eyelet trim to the opposite long edge of the aida cloth.

Figure C

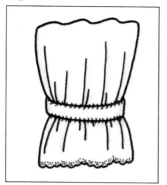

Figure D

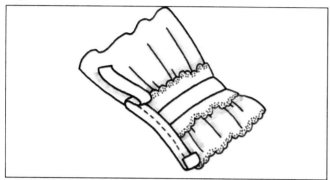

Figure E

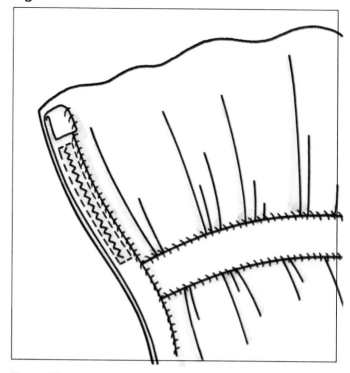

Figure F

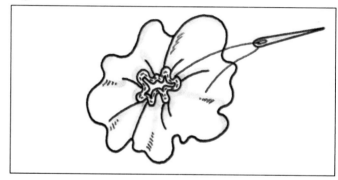

4. Run a line of basting stitches just inside the seam line on one long edge of the piece of eyelet fabric. Pull up the threads to form even gathers, until the edge measures 15 inches long.

5. Pin the gathered fabric to the aida cloth, over the eyelet you attached in step 3. Place the gathered edge of the fabric even with the raw edge of the aida cloth strip, right sides together. Stitch along the seam line. Turn the eyelet trim and fabric outward, and press all seam allowances toward the aida cloth.

6. A length of seam binding will cover all of the raw edges and seam allowances which have been turned to the wrong side of the aida cloth. Cut a 15-inch length of seam binding and press it open. Press a hem allowance to the wrong side of the binding along each long edge, so that it is 1¾ inches wide. Pin the binding to the aida cloth assembly, placing wrong sides together, so that the pressed edges of the binding lie along the stitched seams on each long edge of the aida cloth. Whipstitch along each long edge of the binding as shown in **Figure C**.

Finishing the side edges

1. Cut a 16¾-inch length of seam binding. Press the binding open, and press a ½-inch hem allowance to the wrong side on each short end.

2. With right sides together, pin the binding along one side edge of the bonnet (from the front of the wide eyelet trim to the end of the eyelet fabric), placing the center fold of the binding along the seam line (**Figure D**). Stitch along the fold line, being careful to keep the eyelet trims flat as you stitch over them.

3. Refold the binding along the seam line, and press the binding and seam allowance to the wrong side of the bonnet.

4. Cut a 3-inch length of elastic. Sandwich the elastic between the two seam binding layers as shown in **Figure E**, and stitch through all thicknesses (eyelet fabric, elastic, and both binding layers), across the front end of the elastic.

5. Stretch the elastic out so that the free end reaches to a point approximately 1½ inches from the rear edges of the eyelet fabric and binding. Use a wide zigzag setting on your machine to stitch along the entire center length of the elastic, through all thicknesses, keeping the elastic stretched as you stitch (**Figure E**). Stitch across the elastic at the end as you did at the front.

6. Whipstitch the open edges of the binding to the bonnet.

7. Cut an 8-inch length of narrow eyelet trim and a 21-inch length of satin ribbon. The ribbon will serve as a tie. The eyelet will be gathered into a circle to look like a flower, and will be used to anchor the tie to one end of the aida cloth strip.

Figure H

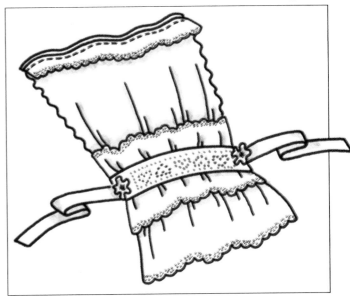

Figure G

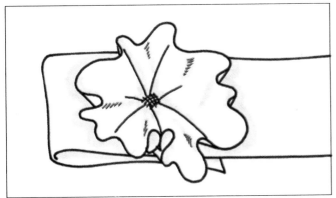

Figure I

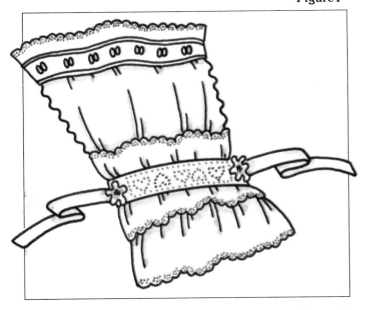

Figure J

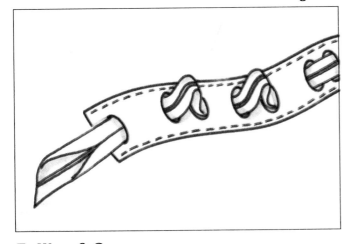

8. Press a narrow allowance to the wrong side on each short raw end of the eyelet. Run a line of basting stitches along the bound edge of the eyelet, and pull up tight gathers so that the eyelet forms a circle with the gathered edge in the center (**Figure F**). Take a few stitches to secure the circle.

9. Fold a 1½-inch allowance to the wrong side on one end of the ribbon. Pin the folded end of the ribbon to the aida cloth strip on the bonnet, near one side seam, and pin the eyelet flower on top (**Figure G**). The center of the eyelet flower should be approximately 1 inch from the side edge. Take several hand stitches through all thicknesses at the center of the flower, using pink embroidery floss. Cut the opposite end of the ribbon at an angle.

10. Repeat all of the procedures in this section to finish the opposite side of the bonnet.

Finishing the back edge

1. Cut a 36-inch length of narrow eyelet trim and pin the bound edge ¼ inch from the back raw edge of the eyelet fabric, placing right sides together (**Figure H**). The scalloped eyelet edge should extend in toward the center of the bonnet. Turn the ends of the eyelet to the wrong side. Stitch along the seam line, then turn the eyelet outward and press the seam allowance toward the bonnet.

2. Pin the ribbon eyelet along the turned back edge of the eyelet fabric, placing the wrong side of the ribbon eyelet against the right side of the fabric (**Figure I**). Turn the ends of the ribbon eyelet to the wrong side, and stitch along each long edge.

3. Cut both ends of the remaining length of satin ribbon at an angle. Weave the ribbon through the ribbon eyelet, threading it in and out of the oval-shaped openings as shown in **Figure J**. When you reach the end, pull the ribbon through until the ends are of equal length. Pull up the ribbon ends to gather the back of the bonnet tightly, and tie them in a bow.

To Wear & Carry

113

Lounging Slippers

Treat your feet to a new pair of slippers. These are made on a very simple pattern, and are a real breeze to complete once the cross-stitch is done.

Materials

Two rectangular pieces of pale blue 14-count aida cloth, each 6 x 6½ inches.

½ yard of burgundy-colored fleece fabric.

⅛ yard of thin leather (or substitute the rubber fabric used for the foot soles on infant sleepers.)

¼ yard of buckram or other heavy stiffening fabric.

Embroidery floss in medium blue, deep pink, purple, charcoal gray, and medium green.

Tapestry and regular needles, pins, burgundy thread, steam iron, sewing machine, pattern paper.

Cross-stitch

A color-coded cross-stitch graph for the floral design is provided in **Figure A**. Stitch the design in the center of each aida rectangle. Press the completed work on the wrong side of the fabric, using a steam iron.

Figure A

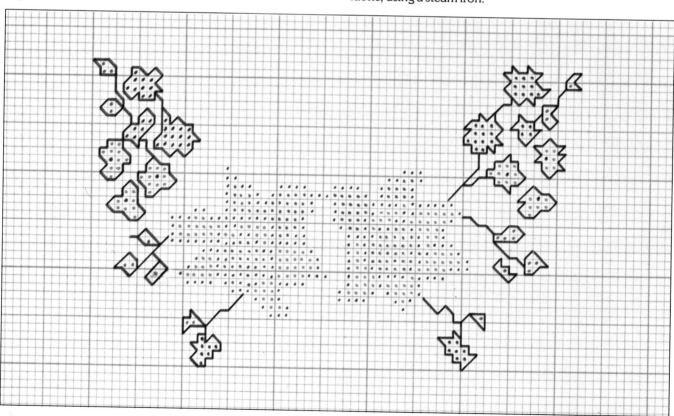

114

SOLE

TOE

Cutting the pieces

1. Scale drawings for the slipper patterns are given in **Figure B**. Enlarge the drawings to full-size paper patterns. (The sole pattern is for the left foot. Turned upside down, it will serve as a pattern for the sole of the right foot.) Before you cut the pieces, place the sole pattern on the floor and stand on it to be sure the slippers will fit. (Don't forget that the pattern includes a ½-inch seam allowance all the way around.) You may also wish to pin the paper toe pattern in place over the sole pattern to check it for proper fit. If necessary, cut the patterns smaller or draw and cut larger ones, maintaining the shape of the original drawings.

2. For each slipper, cut one sole and one toe from burgundy fleece. Cut an additional sole for the bottom of the slipper from leather. Cut two inner sole pieces for each slipper from buckram, using the same pattern.

3. Center the toe pattern over the cross-stitched design on one aida cloth rectangle. Cut the cloth to the shape of the pattern. Cut the remaining aida cloth in the same manner.

4. The edges of the slippers are bound with bias binding cut from the burgundy fleece. For each slipper, cut and piece together 2-inch-wide bias strips to form one continuous strip 2 x 25 inches.

Figure C

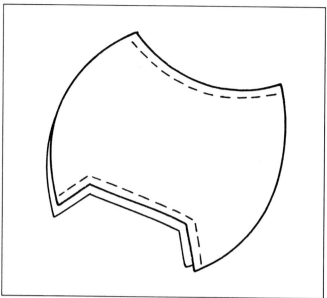

Assembly

1. Begin by assembling the pieces of the left slipper. Place the leather bottom sole wrong side up on a flat surface. Stack the two buckram inner soles and then the fleece sole (right side up) on top. Pin and baste the four layers together along the seam line.

2. Pin the aida and fleece toes right sides together, and stitch the seams along the curved top and bottom edges (**Figure C**). Leave both side edges open and unstitched. Clip the curves and turn the stitched toe assembly right side out. Baste the two layers together along the side seam lines. Pin the assembled toe over the basted sole assembly, matching side seam lines.

3. Press a ½-inch allowance to the wrong side along one long raw edge of the bias binding strip. Pin the bias strip around the edge on top of the slipper, placing right sides together. The unfolded long raw edge of the binding should be even with the raw edge of the slipper assembly, and the folded edge should extend toward the center. Overlap the ends of the binding at the center of the inner edge. Turn the final end of the binding strip to the wrong side, and stitch all the way around the slipper through all thicknesses of fabric (**Figure D**).

4. Turn the strip outward, folding it over the raw edge of the slipper, and pin the folded edge to the bottom of the leather sole, easing the curves. Whipstitch all the way around the folded edge (**Figure E**).

5. Repeat steps 1 through 4, using the pieces for the right-hand slipper.

Figure D

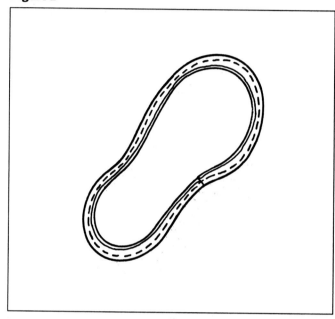

Figure E

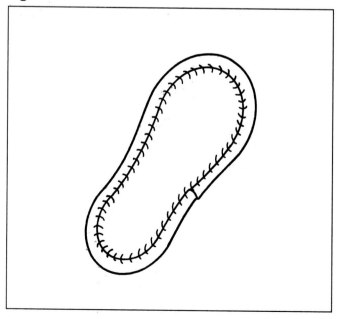

Garment Bag

A garment bag is handy for travel or for storing fine clothing at home. The cross-stitched monogram adds a personalized touch.

Materials

You can purchase a garment bag and simply add the cross-stitched monogram, or make this fully-lined model.

For the monogram, you'll need:

5½ x 7-inch piece of tan 14-count aida cloth.

Chocolate-brown embroidery floss.

⅝ yard of chocolate-brown corded piping.

Tapestry and regular needles, pins, scissors, sewing machine, steam iron, brown thread.

To make the garment bag, you'll need the following additional materials:

2¾ yards of 36-inch-wide light brown fabric for the outer bag. We used a nylon/cotton blend.

2¾ yards of 36-inch-wide lining fabric to coordinate with the outer fabric.

7⅜ yards of chocolate-brown corded piping.

¾ yard of nylon fastener stripping.

4¼ x 14-inch piece of thin beige leather or vinyl.

Pattern paper.

Cross-stitch

You'll find alphabet cross-stitch graphs in **Figure A**. Refer to the larger alphabet as you work the initial letter of your last name in the center of the aida cloth. Refer to the smaller alphabet as you work the initial letters of your first and middle names (or first and maiden names) on either side of the larger initial. Press your finished work gently on the wrong side of the fabric.

Figure A

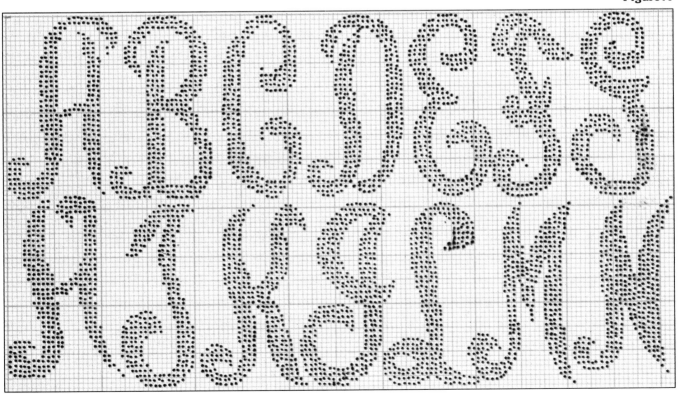

Figure A

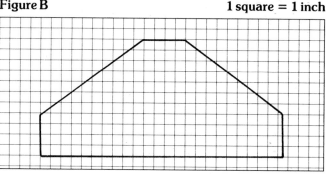

Figure C

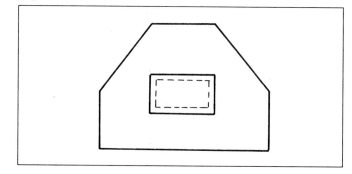

Figure D　　　　　　　**Figure E**

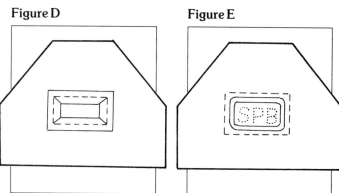

Cutting the outer pieces

The outer bag is cut and assembled first, and then the lining is added.

1. Cut the following pieces from the outer bag fabric: two lower front pieces, each 13½ x 29 inches; one back piece, 23½ x 39½ inches; two side gussets, each 5½ x 45½ inches; two top gussets, each 5½ x 3 inches; and one bottom gusset, 5½ x 19 inches.

2. A scale drawing for the upper front piece is provided in **Figure B**. Enlarge the drawing to a full-size paper pattern and cut one upper front piece from the bag fabric. Now place the pattern over one end of the large back piece that you cut in step 1, and cut the fabric to the shape of the pattern.

Attaching the monogram

1. The cross-stitched monogram is bordered with piping and framed in a window at the center of the upper front bag piece. To create the window, first cut a 6½ x 8-inch facing piece from the outer bag fabric. Pin it to the upper front piece approximately 1¼ inches from the lower edge and centered between the sides, placing right sides together. Stitch through both thicknesses 1 inch from each edge of the facing piece (**Figure C**).

2. To "open" the window, cut away both layers of fabric inside the stitching lines, cutting ½ inch from each line. Clip the corners up to the stitching (**Figure D**). Turn the seam allowances to the wrong side of the upper front piece, along the stitching lines, and press. Turn what's left of the facing piece through the open window to the wrong side of the upper front piece, and press. The edges of the window opening are now finished.

3. Place the cross-stitched aida cloth right side up on a flat surface. Pin a length of corded piping around the edges of the aida cloth, overlapping the ends at a corner. The corded edge of the piping should extend in toward the center of the cloth, and the raw edges should be even with the raw edges of the cloth.

4. Place the aida cloth under the window opening in the upper front bag piece to check for proper placement of the piping. With the monogram centered in the window, the corded edge of the piping should border the finished edges of the window. Adjust the piping if necessasy, and baste it to the aida cloth. Pin the aida cloth in place under the window opening and topstitch through all thicknesses, close to the finished window edges (**Figure E**). Use a zipper foot attachment to stitch close to the cording.

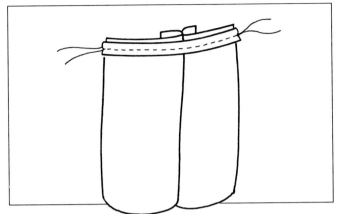

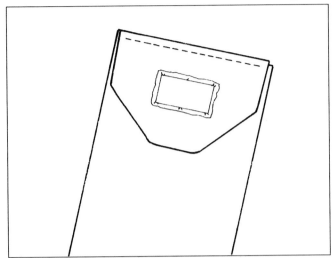

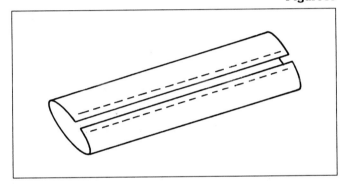

Figure I

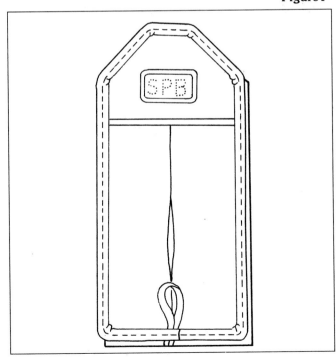

Assembling the bag front

Note: All seam allowances are ½ inch unless otherwise specified in the instructions.

1. Begin by assembling the front of the bag. On each of the two lower front pieces, turn a ½-inch hem allowance to the wrong side of the fabric along one long edge, and press.

2. Place the two lower front pieces right side up on a flat surface, overlapping the folded edges by 2¼ inches. (This will be the vertical front opening of the bag.) Pin a length of corded piping along the short upper edges, so that the raw edge of the piping is even with the raw edges of the fabric and the corded edge of the piping points toward the bottom of the fabric pieces (**Figure F**). Baste the piping in place.

3. Pin the upper front piece right side down over the lower front pieces as shown in **Figure G**. (The piping will be sandwiched between.) Stitch through all thicknesses, using a zipper foot attachment, and press the seam open.

4. Place the assembled bag front right side up on a flat surface and pin a length of piping around the entire outer edge, overlapping the ends at the bottom center. The raw edge of the piping should be even with the raw edge of the fabric, and the corded edge of the piping should extend in toward the center of the bag front.

5. To make the bottom loop, cut a 1½ x 14-inch piece of leather or vinyl. Fold each long edge to the wrong side, so that they meet in the center, and stitch (**Figure H**). Fold the leather strip in a horseshoe shape and insert the ends between the piping and fabric at the bottom center of the bag front (**Figure I**). The right side of the strip should be against the right side of the bag fabric. Baste all the way around the bag front, close to the piping cord.

Figure J

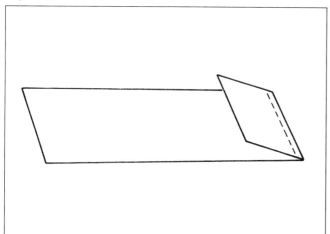

Figure K

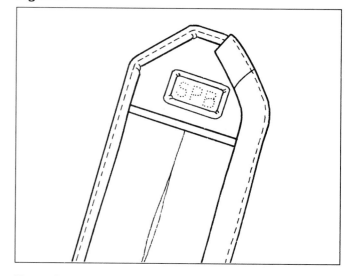

Figure L

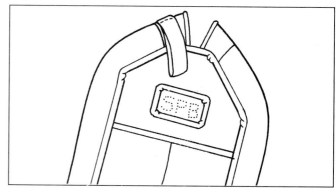

Adding the gussets

1. Pin one top gusset piece and one side gusset piece right sides together aligning two short ends, and stitch them together along one 5½-inch end (**Figure J**). Press the seam open. Pin a length of corded piping along the free short end of the top gusset on the right side of the fabric. (Raw edges of piping and fabric should be even.) Stitch as close as possible to the cording, using a zipper foot attachment, and press the raw edges of the piping and fabric to the wrong side along the seam line. Turn and press a ½-inch allowance to the wrong side of the fabric on the remaining short raw edge of the side gusset. Repeat these procedures to assemble the remaining top and side gusset pieces.

2. Pin one assembled top/side gusset piece to the bag front, placing right sides together so that the corded end of the gusset is at the top center of the bag front. The piping basted to the bag front will be sandwiched between. The raw edges of gusset, piping, and bag should be even, and the width of the gusset assembly should extend in toward the center of the bag (**Figure K**). Pin the remaining top/side gusset assembly along the opposite edge of the bag front.

3. Pin the bottom gusset to the lower edge of the bag front, overlapping the ends of the two side gussets. Stitch all the way around the edge of the bag front through all thicknesses, using a zipper foot attachment so that the stitching will be as close as possible to the corded edge of the piping.

4. Turn the gusset sections outward and press the seams open. Topstitch along the folded lower end of each side gusset, through the side and bottom gussets.

Adding the handle and back

1. To make the handle, first cut a 2¾ x 7-inch piece of bag fabric and an identical piece of leather fabric. Place the two pieces right sides together and stitch ½ inch from each edge, leaving one short edge open and unstitched.

2. Turn the handle right side out and press. Fold it in half lengthwise, placing the leather on the inside, and pin the unstitched short end to the right side of one top gusset section. The raw edges of the handle should be even with the back raw edge of the gusset, and the folded edge of the handle should be even with the top/side gusset seam (**Figure L**). Baste the handle in place along the seam line.

3. Pin a length of piping around the edge of the bag back piece as you did the front. Baste.

4. Place the assembled bag front (with gusset) right side up on a flat surface. Place the bag back right side down on top of the front. Pin the bag back to the long raw edge of the gusset assembly (the piping will be sandwiched between), placing right sides together and raw edges even. Stitch. Press the seams, clip all corners, and turn the bag right side out through the front opening.

5. Whipstitch the two halves of the folded handle together along the short end and approximately 2 inches down the long open edge. Whipstitch the piped center edges of the top gussets together at front and back, leaving a 1½-inch opening at the center to accomodate one or more hanger tops.

To Wear & Carry

Assembling the lining

1. Cut identical pieces for the lining as you did for the outer bag (all steps under "Cutting the outer pieces"). You need not cut the two top gusset pieces, but cut the side gussets 2½ inches longer than specified.

2. Place the bottom gusset and one side gusset right sides together and stitch the seam across one short end. Attach the remaining side gusset to the opposite end of the bottom gusset, and press all seams open.

3. Stitch the gusset assembly to the back lining, placing right sides together and matching the bottom center points. Leave a few inches at the upper end of each side gusset unstitched. Turn the upper short edge of each side gusset to the wrong side, so that the folded ends come within ¼ inch of meeting at the top center, and press. Finish stitching the gussets to the back lining at the top.

To Wear & Carry

4. Place the two lower front lining pieces right side up, overlapping the center edges by about 3 inches. Place the upper front lining piece right side down over them (as you did for the outer bag), and adjust the overlap so that the width of the bottom section matches the upper piece. Pin and then stitch the seam, leaving the center 4 inches open and unstitched (**Figure M**).

5. Pin the front lining assembly to the free edge of the lining gusset, placing right sides together and matching top centers. Stitch all the way around, leaving a 4-inch opening at the bottom center where the lower front pieces overlap.

Installing the lining

1. Turn the outer bag inside out and insert a sturdy hanger. Hang the bag at a convenient working height. Place the lining (right side out) over the bag.

2. On each overlapped edge at the center front, fold the raw edge of the lining piece to the wrong side and whipstitch it to the folded edge of the outer bag piece. Whipstitch the edges of the 4-inch openings that you previously left in the seams at the top and bottom of the center front.

3. Whipstitch the folded top center edges of the lining gusset to the piping.

4. Separate the halves of the nylon fastener strip and whipstitch one half to each side of the center front overlap.

To carry

Fold the bottom of the garment bag upward and wrap the leather loop around the hanger top. Slip the hanger top inside the folded handle at the top of the bag. You'll find this a comfortable and convenient way to carry the bag.

Cross-Stitch Keeper

Organize your cross-stitch trappings in this attractive carrying case. Opened and placed over the arm of a chair, it becomes a convenient work center.

Materials

1½ yards of burgundy fleece fabric.

Small quantities of three different calico print fabrics, all in shades of burgundy. We used ½ yard of one print, ¼ yard of a second, and a 4¼ x 6¾-inch piece of a third.

1⅛ yards of white fabric-covered cording.

12½ x 33½-inch piece of quilt batting.

Small quantity of polyester fiberfill.

3¼ x 6¾-inch piece of ivory-colored 14-count aida cloth.

2¾ x 12¼-inch piece of cardboard.

Two flat pearl buttons, each ¾ inch in diameter.

Embroidery floss in burgundy and pink.

1-yard length of nylon fastening strip.

Thread to match the fabrics.

Tapestry and regular needles, pins, sewing machine, scissors, steam iron, measuring tape.

Cross-stitch

A stitching graph for the "I love x-stitch" message is provided in **Figure A**. Stitch the message in the center of the aida

Figure A

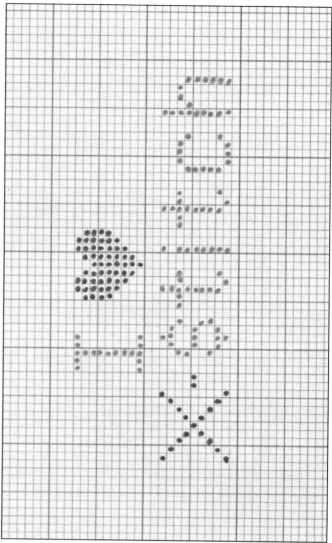

cloth. Staystitch ¼ inch from each edge, to keep the cloth from fraying.

Cutting the pieces

Since all of the pieces are simple rectangles we have not provided patterns. We suggest that you label all pieces as you cut them, to avoid confusion.

1. Cut the following pieces from fleece: one cover and one lining, each 13½ x 34½ inches; one handle 2¼ x 12 inches; one flap lining 7 x 12½ inches; one pin cushion lining 4¼ x 13½ inches; one upper pocket lining 7½ x 13¾ inches; and one lower pocket lining 11¼ x 13¾ inches.

2. Cut the following pieces from the largest piece of calico: one flap 7 x 12½ inches; one pin cushion 4¼ x 13½ inches; one upper pocket 7½ x 13¾ inches; patchwork piece number four, 4½ x 8¾ inches; and patchwork piece number two, 4½ x 6½ inches.

3. Cut the following pieces from ¼ yard of calico: patchwork piece number three, 3¼ x 10¼ inches; and patchwork piece number five, 3½ x 13¾ inches.

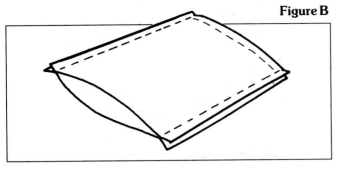

Figure B

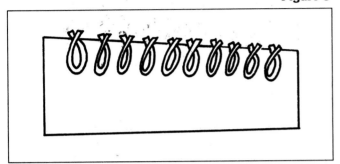

Figure C

Figure D

Figure E

Figure F

Figure G

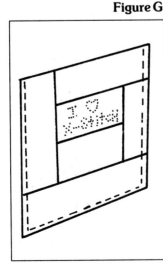

Making the flap and pin cushion

The inner workings of the cross-stitch keeper consist of a long thin pin cushion, two pockets (one of which has a patchwork front), and a flap that can be fastened to the lining to keep threads and flosses from getting all wadded up in a mess. The inner pieces are made first, and are sewn into the lined cover. All seam allowances are ½ inch.

1. To make the flap, pin the calico flap and fleece flap lining pieces right sides together. Stitch the seams on the two long edges and one short edge, leaving the remaining short edge open and unstitched (**Figure B**). Clip the corners and turn the flap right side out. Press gently. Baste the open raw edges together, just inside the seam line.

2. Begin work on the pin cushion by making ten loops that will be sewn into one side. The loops are meant to hold your stitching floss, and are made from fabric-covered cording. Cut ten pieces of cording, each 4 inches long. Fold each piece in half, crossing the ends and tacking them together to form a loop.

3. Place the calico pin cushion piece right side up on a flat surface. Place the loops at evenly spaced intervals along one 13½-inch edge (**Figure C**), leaving about 2 inches of space between the outer loops and the corners of the fabric. The raw edges of the loops should be even with the edge of the fabric, and the looped ends should extend in toward the center. Baste the loops in place, just inside the seam line.

4. Pin the fleece pin cushion lining right side down over the calico piece. (The loops will be sandwiched between.) Stitch the seams on both long edges, leaving the short edges open and unstitched.

5. Turn the pin cushion right side out and stuff it with fiberfill. Baste across each short end, along the seam line.

Making the lower and upper pockets

1. The lower pocket has a patchwork front, which includes the cross-stitched aida cloth, and a fleece lining. A diagram of the patchwork front is provided in **Figure D**. The numbers shown on the patchwork pieces indicate the order in which they are assembled, and correspond with the labels given them when they were cut. The uncut 4¼ x 6¾-inch piece of calico serves as patchwork piece number one.

2. Place the cross-stitched aida cloth right side up on a flat surface. Place patchwork piece number one right side down over the aida cloth, with lower edges even. Pin and then stitch the seam along the lower edge (**Figure E**). Press open.

3. Place patchwork piece number two right side down over the aida cloth and the first patchwork piece. Pin and then stitch the seam along the right-hand edge. Press open. Follow the same procedures to attach patchwork pieces three, four, and five.

4. Pin the assembled patchwork pocket front to the fleece lower pocket lining, placing right sides together. Stitch only the seam along the upper edge, leaving the remaining three edges open and unstitched (**Figure F**). Turn the pieces so that the wrong sides are together and press. Baste the open edges together, just inside the seam line (**Figure G**).

5. Follow the procedures described in step 4 to assemble the upper pocket, using the calico upper pocket and fleece upper pocket lining pieces.

Figure H

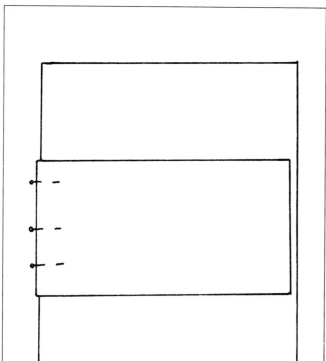

Figure I

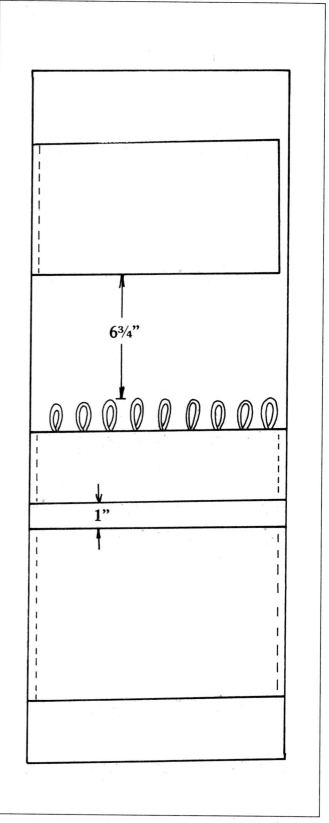

6¾"

1"

Assembly

1. Place the large fleece lining piece right side up on a flat surface. Pin the flap, calico side up, on top of the lining 4½ inches from one end (**Figure H**). The raw edges of the flap should be even with the side edge of the lining. Baste along the seam line. The opposite end of the flap will be held in place with nylon fastening material. For the time being, fold the free short end of the flap back over itself and pin it in place temporarily, so that it won't get caught when the seam is sewn.

2. Pin and baste the upper pocket and pin cushion to the lining (**Figure I**), with calico sides up. Place the looped edge of the pin cushion 6¾ inches from the flap, and place the pocket 1 inch from the pin cushion.

3. Pin and baste the patchwork lower pocket to the lining in the same manner, patchwork side up. Place the bottom edge of the pocket even with the bottom edge of the lining. (The lower pocket will overlap the upper pocket by several inches.) To divide the lower and upper pockets into large and small sections, topstitch through all layers along the right-hand edge of patchwork piece number 4.

4. Pin the large fleece cover piece right side down over this assembly. Stitch the seams through all thicknesses along the two long edges and the lower short edge (the edge that includes the pocket). Leave the short edge at the top of the assembly open and unstitched.

5. Clip the corners and turn the assembly right side out. Press the seam allowances to the inside on the raw edges.

6. Place the assembled cross-stitch keeper over the quilt batting, and trim the batting to size if necessary. Insert the batting between the cover and lining.

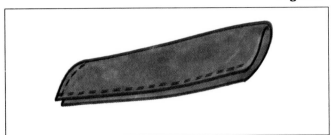

Figure J

Figure K

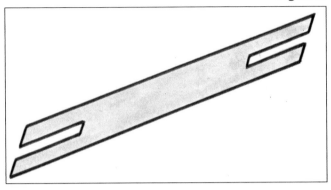

Figure L

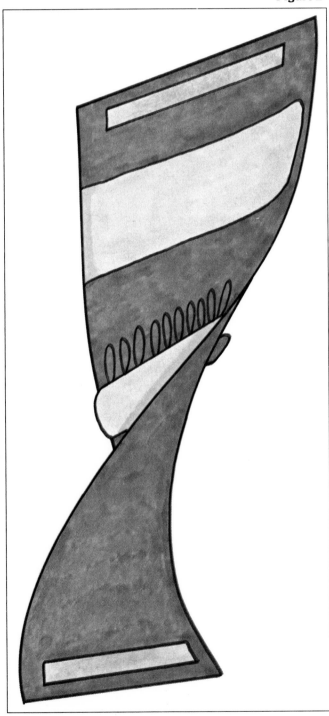

Adding the handle and fasteners

1. Fold the fleece handle piece in half lengthwise and stitch the seam along one short edge and the long edge (**Figure J**). Turn the handle right side out and press gently. Press the seam allowance to the inside on the open end and whipstitch the edges together.

2. The cardboard will serve as a support for the handle when the cross-stitch keeper is being carried. But because it is somewhat difficult (to say the least) to stitch through cardboard, slots are cut to accommodate the button stitching. Cut a slot into each end of the piece of cardboard as shown in **Figure K**. The slots should measure approximately ¼ x 2½ inches.

3. Insert the cardboard into the open end of the cross-stitch keeper, between the batting and lining layers. Push it along until it is aligned beneath the pin cushion. Place the handle on the outside of the fleece cover, over the center line of the cardboard. The ends of the handle should lie about 1 inch inside the edges of the cover (it will be slightly humped up in the center). Pin the ends of the handle in place. Sew a button near each end of the handle, stitching all the way through to the pin cushion lining, and passing through the slots in the cardboard.

4. Whipstitch the open edges of the fleece cover and lining together.

5. Cut a 10-inch length of the nylon fastener strip and separate the sides. Stitch one piece to the inside of the lining, along the end nearest the flap. Stitch the other piece to the outside of the cover, approximately 2 inches from the opposite end (**Figure L**).

6. Stitch lengths of nylon fastener to the flap also, to help keep your floss from tangling. Cut five pieces of the fastener strip, each 5 inches long. Sew the halves of one strip to the flap lining and cover lining at the free end of the flap. Sew the remaining strips at even intervals along the flap. You can hang embroidery flosses from the loops attached to the pin cushion, and guide the ends down into these separate compartments.

Mousie Ballerina Tote Bag

This fashionable tote is large enough to carry a weekend's necessities, an infant's trappings, or a ballerina's belongings. The cross-stitched design on the exterior pocket depicts several thin mousie ladies in classic ballet posture, and the demure Miss Plump of the mouse world.

Figure A

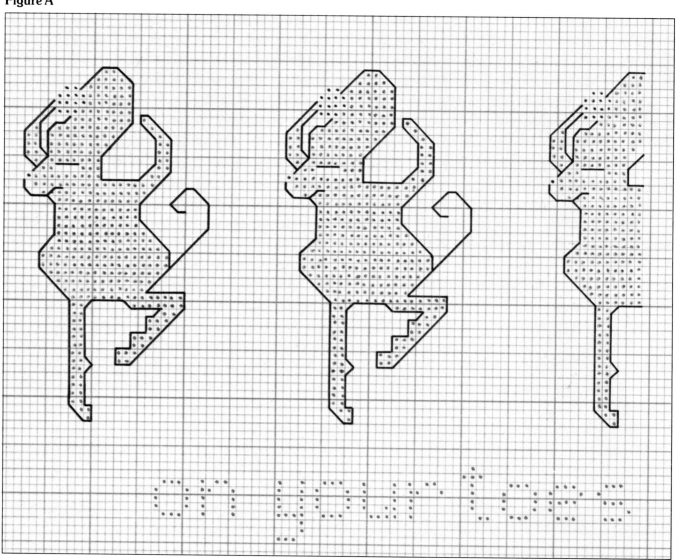

Materials

1½ yards of pre-quilted pink-and-white gingham fabric.

2½ yards of burgundy-colored fleece fabric.

1 yard of ⅛-inch-wide pink satin ribbon.

1¼ yards of ½-inch-wide pink lace trim.

10½ x 14-inch piece of pale pink 14-count aida cloth.

Stiffening material (optional). Because this tote is so large, it needs a little help if you want it to stand up straight all by itself. You can accomplish this by adding stiffening material between the bottom of the bag and the lining, and in-side the divider sleeve. One layer of thick quilt batting or several layers of very stiff interfacing or buckram will do the job. The bottom area measures 4 x 20 inches, and the divider sleeve measures 4 x 13 inches.

Embroidery floss in dark gray, light gray, pink, and burgundy.

White sewing thread and needle, tapestry needle, scissors, embroidery hoop, pins, sewing machine, pattern paper, and a small quantity of polyester fiberfill.

Cross-stitch

You'll find a color-coded cross-stitch graph for the mousies and motto in **Figure A**. Work the design on the aida cloth, and set it aside until you get to "Making the pocket."

Figure A

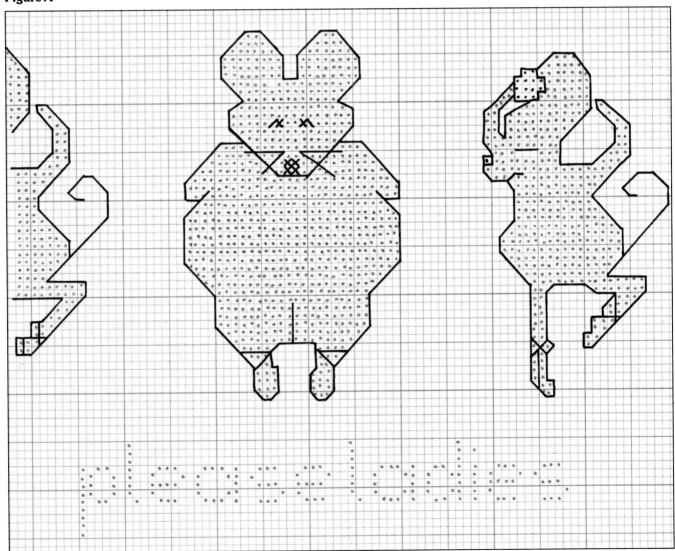

Figure B

Figure C

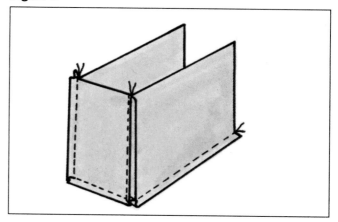

Figure D

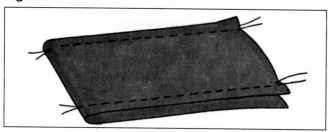

Figure E

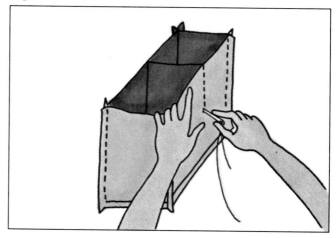

Figure F

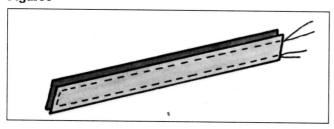

Making the bag, lining, and strap

Note: All seam allowances are ½ inch unless otherwise specified.

1. The outer bag consists of a front and a back panel, each 14 x 21 inches; two identical side panels, 14 x 5 inches; and one bottom panel, 21 x 5 inches. Cut these pieces from the pink-and-white gingham.

2. Cut identical pieces from burgundy fleece for the bag lining. Cut one divider sleeve from fleece, 27 x 5 inches.

3. The strap pieces measure 36 x 2½ inches. Cut two straps from gingham and two from fleece.

4. Begin by assembling the gingham pieces to form the outer bag. Pin the bottom panel to the front panel, placing right sides together (**Figure B**), and stitch. Turn the bottom panel out and press the seam open. Pin the back panel to the opposite long edge of the bottom panel, placing right sides together. Stitch the seam and press it open.

5. Pin one side panel to the front, bottom, and back as shown in **Figure C**, placing right sides together and easing the side panel to fit at the corners. Stitch the seam and clip the corners. Attach the remaining side panel to the opposite side, press all seams, and turn the bag right side out.

6. Repeat steps 4 and 5 using the fleece pieces to form the bag lining. Press all seams, and leave the lining inside out.

7. To make the center divider, fold the divider sleeve piece in half widthwise, right sides together, and stitch the side seams as shown in **Figure D**. Turn right side out and press gently.

8. If you wish to add stiffening, cut one piece of batting (or several pieces of buckram) 4 x 13 inches. Insert the stiffening into the divider sleeve. Now turn the raw edges of the sleeve to the inside (whether or not you have added stiffening), and whipstitch the opening edges together.

9. Place the stitched divider sleeve inside the lining and whipstitch it in place along both sides and the lower edge, as shown in **Figure E**. This is quite simple to do if you work from the outside of the lining and pinch the lining up into a ridge, pulling the divider edge into the ridge, with each stitch.

10. The tote bag will have two straps. Place one gingham strap piece and one fleece strap piece right sides together, and stitch close to two long edges and one short edge (**Figure F**), leaving the remaining short edge open and unstitched. Clip the corners, turn the stitched strap right side out, and press. Turn the remaining raw edges to the inside, press, and whipstitch the opening edges together. Repeat to form the second strap, using the remaining gingham and fleece strap pieces. The bag, lining, and straps will be assembled after the cross-stitched pocket has been added.

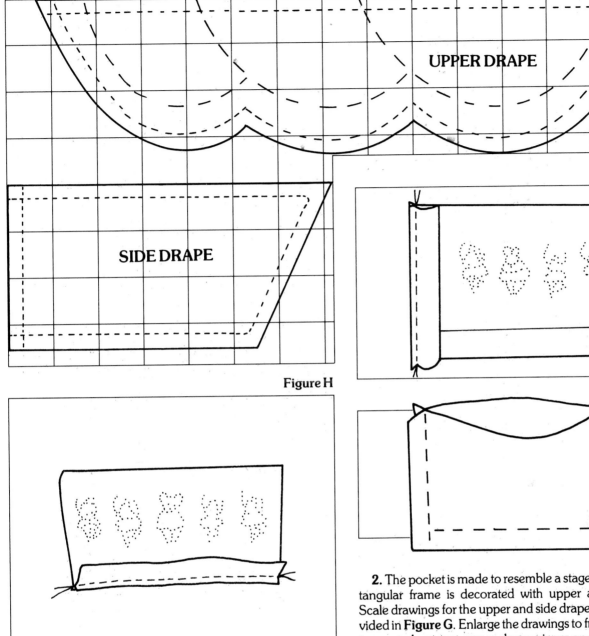

Figure G

UPPER DRAPE

SIDE DRAPE

Figure I

Figure H

Figure J

Making the pocket

1. The cross-stitched aida cloth forms the pocket. Tie a small pink satin ribbon bow for each of the dancing mice. Hand stitch a bow at each thin mousie's neck, and between the not-so-thin mousie's ears. For the skirts, cut four 8-inch lengths and one 10-inch length of pink lace trim. Run a line of basting stitches close to the straight edge of each length of lace. Pull up tight gathers, and tie off the thread. Tack a short gathered length to the waist edge of each thin mousie. The longer gathered length will, naturally, serve as the not-so-thin mousie's skirt.

2. The pocket is made to resemble a stage curtain. The rectangular frame is decorated with upper and side drapes. Scale drawings for the upper and side drape patterns are provided in **Figure G**. Enlarge the drawings to full-size paper patterns, and cut two upper drape pieces and four side drape pieces from fleece. Cut one frame piece, 14 x 2 inches; and two frame pieces, each 11½ x 2½ inches, from fleece. Cut one pocket lining, 11½ x 17 inches, from the same fabric.

3. Place the cross-stitched aida cloth right side up on a flat surface. Place the longer frame piece right side down over the aida cloth, with lower edges even (**Figure H**). Stitch, turn the frame piece out, and press the seam open.

4. Follow the same procedures to attach one shorter frame piece to each side of the aida cloth and longer frame assembly (**Figure I**). Press the seams open.

5. Pin the pocket lining to the framed aida cloth placing right sides together, and stitch the side and bottom seams, leaving the upper edge open and unstitched (**Figure J**). Turn the stitched pocket panel right side out and press gently.

To Wear & Carry

131

Figure K

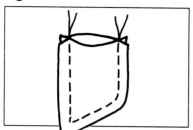

Figure L

Figure M

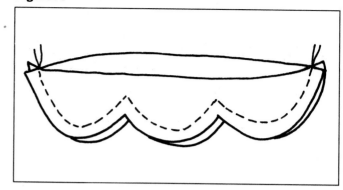

Figure N

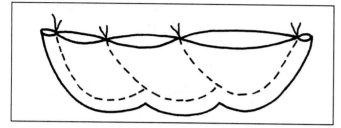

Figure O

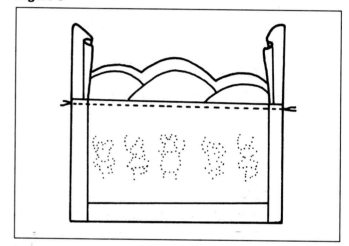

Figure P

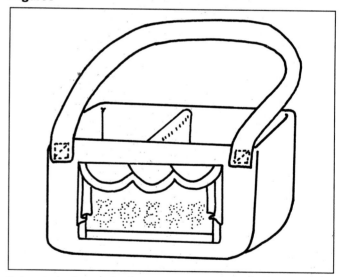

6. To make each side section of the stage curtain, pin two side drape pieces right sides together and stitch close to both long edges and the angled short edge, leaving the straight upper edge open and unstitched (**Figure K**). Turn the stitched side drape right side out and press gently. Fold the drape into a lengthwise pleat (**Figure L**), and tack the pleat in place near the lower and upper edges. Repeat this step, using the remaining two side drape pieces.

7. To make the scalloped upper curtain, pin the two upper drape pieces right sides together and stitch close to the long scalloped edge (**Figure M**). Turn the stitched drape right side out, press gently, and stuff lightly with fiberfill. To create the swagged effect, topstitch through all layers along the stitching lines shown in **Figure N** (approximately 1 inch from the scalloped edge, and up to the top edge, following each of the curves).

8. Turn the raw upper edges of the aida cloth and pocket lining to the inside, and press. Place the pocket right side up on a flat surface. With right sides down, insert the raw edges of the side and upper drapes between the aida cloth and lining, as shown in **Figure O**. Insert the edge of the upper drape first, and center it. Insert the side drapes, on top of the upper drape. Stitch close to the upper edge of the pocket through all thicknesses, as shown.

9. Turn the drape sections down over the upper edge of the pocket, and press gently. Tack the drape sections to the pocket and frame.

10. Pin the assembled pocket to the front bag panel, and blindstitch it in place along the sides and bottom.

Final assembly

1. Fold and press the upper raw edges of the outer bag to the inside. If you wish to add stiffening, cut one piece of batting or several pieces of buckram 4 x 20 inches. Place the stiffening inside the bottom of the bag.

2. Insert the lining inside the bag. (The lining should still be inside out, with the divider sleeve stitched inside.) Tack the lining to the bag at the four corners of the bottom panel. Turn the upper raw edges of the lining to the wrong side, so that the lining is even with the bag. Whipstitch the folded upper edges of bag and lining together.

3. Attach the ends of one strap to the top of the front panel, with the gingham side facing outward, as shown in **Figure P**. Attach the ends of the remaining strap to the top of the back panel.

To Wear & Carry

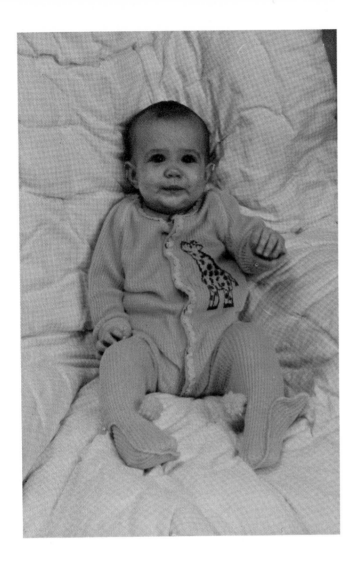

Sleeper Designs

The whimsical designs provided here can be stitched on an infant's sleeper, on any other piece of clothing, or on a wall hanging or other decorator item.

Materials

You'll need waste canvas and embroidery floss for each design you wish to reproduce. The following list of materials includes only the items required to stitch the giraffe design on an infant's sleeper.

One pale turquoise infant's sleeper.
4½ x 6-inch piece of 14-count waste canvas.
1 yard of bright yellow braid trim or rickrack.
Embroidery floss in bright yellow and brown.
Tapestry and regular needles, pins, steam iron, sponge, yellow thread, sewing machine (optional).

To Wear & Carry

Cross-stitch

Pin the waste canvas to the sleeper over the spot where you want the design to appear. Cross-stitch the giraffe design through both the canvas and sleeper fabric, following the color-coded graph provided in **Figure A**.

When you have completed the design, carefully soak the area (using a damp sponge) to soften the canvas, and then remove the canvas threads by pulling them out one by one.

Finishing touches

1. Carefully press the cross-stitched design on the wrong side of the sleeper fabric using a steam setting.

2. Sew braid trim around the neckline and down the center front of the sleeper.

Forever
Clock Calendar

You can call this a "perpetual" calendar clock if you like, but we think "forever" sounds friendlier. Whatever you call it, the battery-powered clock will keep running even when your electricity isn't, and the calendar "pages" are changeable so you can post the one that fits the current month.

Figure A

Materials

2½-foot length of standard 1 x 12-inch pine.

11½ x 15½-inch piece of ¼-inch interior grade plywood.

4½-foot length of ½ x ¾-inch corner molding (or you can cut and rout your own molding from strips of leftover pine 1 x 12 if you have access to a router and are so inclined).

Battery-operated quartz clockwork, including hands. It is not necessary to purchase the numerals for the clock face.

11 x 15-inch piece of ivory-colored 14-count aida cloth.

12 x 13½-inch piece of ivory-colored 22-count aida cloth.

Seven large nylon fastener spots, or seven 3-inch strips.

Navy blue embroidery floss.

Tapestry needle; white glue; scissors; pins; steam iron; drill with a bit to fit the clockwork stem; wood glue; nailset; wood filler; stain; sandpaper; wood sealer; hammer; miter box; small finishing nails; and either a saber saw and a router with a ¼-inch-wide straight bit, or a table saw. The outer edges of the clock case can be routed using a cove bit for a decorative effect.

Cross-stitch

1. The bordered clock face, the initial letters of the weekdays, and the Early American male and female figures are stitched on the large piece of 14-count aida cloth. Cross-stitch graphs are provided in **Figure A**.

Figure A

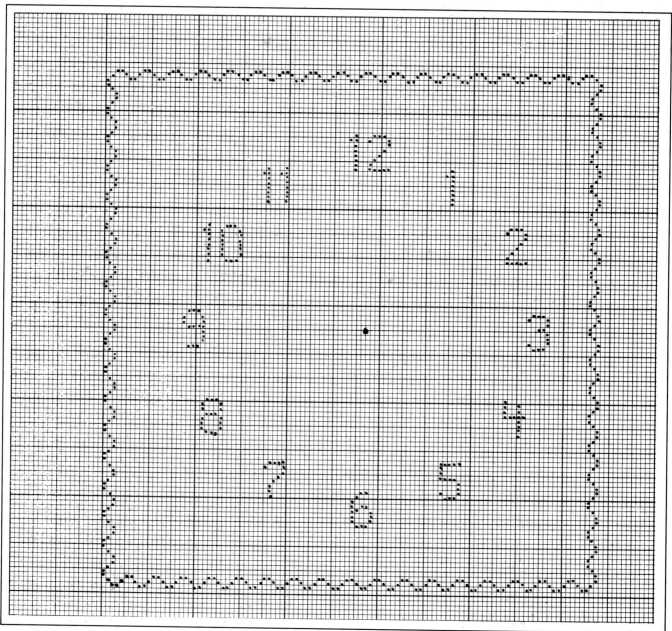

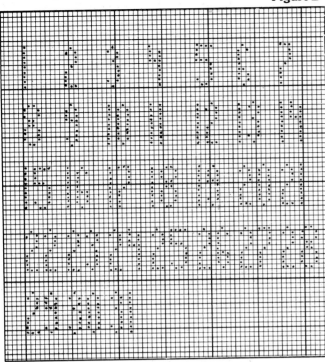

1 square = 1 inch

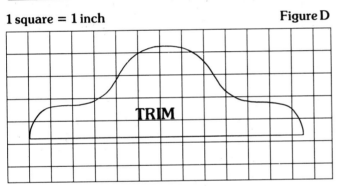

TRIM

2. The calendar "pages" are changeable, and you have a choice of stitching seven or 28 different ones. The easiest method is to stitch a total of seven pages, each with 31 dates, and each with the first day of the month falling on a different day of the week. This way you'll wind up with seven different calendar pages that will accommodate every possible month forever (if you disregard the extra date or dates on the page when a month has fewer than 31 days).

If you opt for this method, cut five pieces of 22-count aida, each 4 x 4½ inches; and two pieces, each 4 x 5¼ inches. The calendar page stitching graph provided in **Figure B** shows the 31 dates arranged properly for a month that begins on Sunday. Stitch this arrangement on one of the smaller pieces of aida. Stitch six additional arrangements on the remaining pieces of aida, using the two larger pieces for the months that begin on Friday and Saturday since these will require an additional row to accommodate all of the dates. Allow a ½-inch hem allowance on all four sides of each piece.

If you prefer to have monthly pages that are correct to the letter, you'll need to purchase an additional ¼ yard of 22-

Figure C

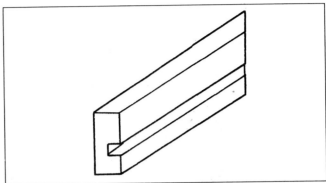

count aida and stitch a total of 28 different pages. In addition to the seven 31-day pages, stitch seven pages with 30 days, seven pages with 28 days, and seven pages with 29 days. This will give you a correct page for every possible monthly arrangement forever.

3. Gently press all of the completed pages and the larger cross-stitched aida cloth on the wrong side of the fabric, using a steam setting.

Attaching the pages

1. Press a ½-inch hem allowance to the wrong side of the fabric on each edge of each calendar page. Glue the hem allowances in place.

2. Place one calendar page on top of the larger cross-stitched aida, just under the initial letters of the weekdays. Adjust it so that the dates fall in the proper places below the letters, and mark the center point on both pieces of aida.

3. Separate the halves of one nylon fastener spot or strip. Glue one half to the large piece of aida and the other half to the back of the calendar page, using the center mark as a placement guide. Separate the remaining fastener spots or strips, and glue a piece to the back of each calendar page. Be sure to use the correct half, or the pages will not stick.

Cutting the clock case pieces

The clock case consists of four rectangular pieces and a decorative top trim piece. The rectangular pieces are grooved on the inside to accommodate the plywood, which serves as a flat backing for the cross-stitched face. Strips of molding hold the aida cloth in place and at the same time create a nicely finished inner edge.

1. Cut the following pieces from the pine 1 x 12: two sides, each 3 x 16⅝ inches; one top and one bottom, each 3 x 12½ inches; and one top trim, 4⅓ x 12½ inches.

2. Miter the ends of the four case pieces (top, bottom, and sides) at a 45 degree angle. On the shorter side of each of these pieces, cut or rout a ¼ x ¼-inch groove, ¾ inch from one long edge (**Figure C**).

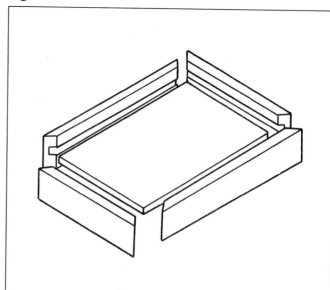

3. A scale drawing for the top trim contour is provided in **Figure D**. Enlarge the drawing to a full-size paper pattern and cut a corresponding contour on the wooden top trim piece.

4. Cut two 15⅛-inch lengths of molding and two 11-inch lengths. Miter the ends at a 45 degree angle.

Assembling the clock

1. Assemble the four case pieces around the plywood rectangle, inserting the edges of the plywood into the grooves (**Figure E**). When you're sure of a proper fit, glue and nail the case pieces together at the corners. Recess the nails and fill the holes with wood filler.

2. Glue and nail the contoured trim piece to the top of the case, flush with the rear edge. (The plywood is closest to the front of the case.)

3. Place the large piece of cross-stitched aida cloth over the plywood, and mark the exact center point of the bordered clock face design. Remove the aida cloth and drill a hole through the plywood at this point.

4. If you wish, rout the front outer edges of the case, using a cove bit. Sand, stain, and seal the clock case and the four mitered lengths of molding. It is not necessary to stain the plywood or the areas on the back which will not show, but it's a good idea to seal them. This will protect the wood from extreme warpage or shrinkage due to absorption and loss of moisture.

5. Cut a small hole in the exact center of the aida cloth clock face. When the case is thoroughly dry, place the cloth over the front of the plywood. Smooth out the cloth and if necessary, trim the edges flush with the inside of the case (**Figure F**). Carefully nail the mitered molding strips inside the case, over the aida cloth edges (**Figure G**). Do not use glue, so you can remove the molding and aida cloth in the event it needs cleaning.

6. Place the clockwork over the hole on the back of the plywood, inserting the stem through the holes in the plywood and aida cloth. Screw on the front parts of the clockwork assembly, including the hands. Follow the manufacturer's installation instructions if they differ from ours.

Figure F

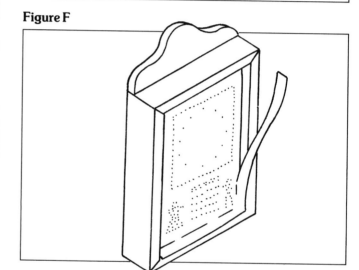

Figure G

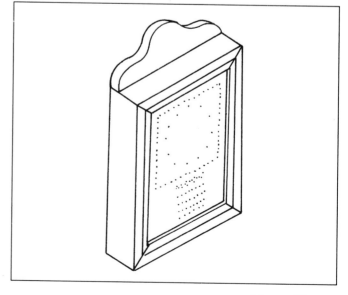

Quilt-Block Chair Seat

This charming chair seat is a cross-stitch reproduction of an early quilt design. Because it reproduces old-style calicoes, it's a good opportunity for using those mountains of multi-colored floss remnants.

Materials

These materials are sufficient to make a quilt-block to fit a 15-inch-diameter round chair seat. If you wish to use a different size chair, you'll need to revise the materials list. The same idea could be used to adapt your own quilt pattern.

2 ¼ yards of unbleached muslin.
10-inch square of ivory-colored 11-count aida cloth.
1 yard of bonded polyester quilt batting, 60 inches wide.
2 yards of wide royal blue bias binding.
2 yards of ½-inch-diameter cotton cord.
Wooden chair with a 15-inch diameter seat.
15-inch-diameter circle of ¼-inch-thick plywood.
Staple gun and ¼-inch-long staples.

Embroidery floss in the colors of your choice. We used deep gold and dusty rose for the center hexagons, and odds and ends of other colors to reproduce the various calicoes.

Tapestry, quilting, and regular needles; pins; scissors; ivory quilting thread; 20-inch quilting hoop; steam iron; and a sewing machine with a zipper foot attachment.

A big help in making this project is a special fabric marking pencil that gives a clear and distinct outline to follow when quilting, but washes out easily with water.

To attach the seat, you will need a screwdriver and four wood screws. The length of the screws will depend on the thickness of your chair seat.

Glue gun and a small quantity of hot-melt adhesive, or use white glue.

Home Decor

139

Figure A

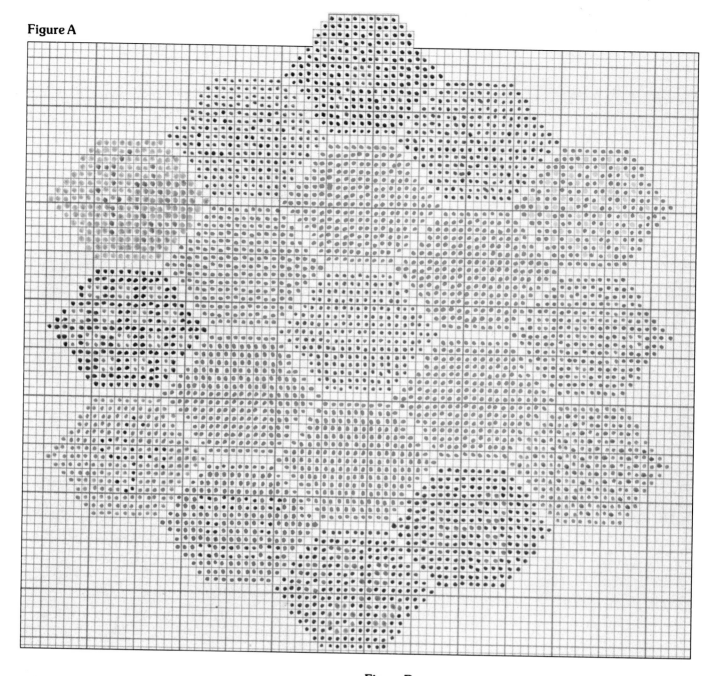

Cross-stitch

A cross-stitch graph for the quilt design is provided in **Figure A**. Reproduce this design on the aida cloth, or graph your own quilt pattern, making sure that it does not exceed 7 inches in diameter. A quilt design that corresponds to the shape of your chair seat (a round design for a round seat, square for square, etc.) is best.

Making the quilted border

1. Cut two 26-inch squares of muslin and pin them together. Draw a 7 ⅝-inch-diameter circle in the center and carefully stitch around the circle, through both layers. To open the window, cut out both layers of fabric in the center of the circle, ½ inch from the stitching line (**Figure B**), and

Figure B

140

Figure C   1 square = 1 inch   **Figure E**

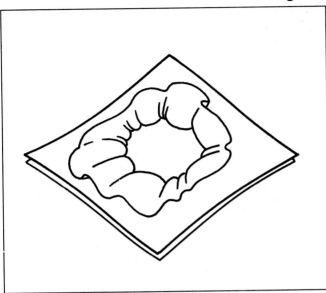

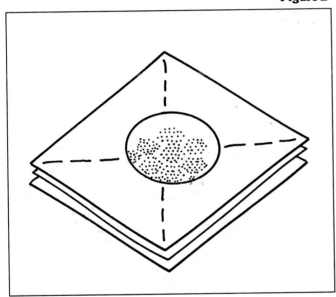

Figure D

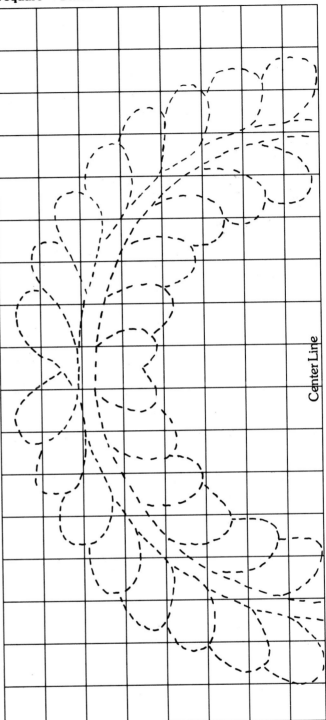

Center Line

clip the seam allowance. Pull one fabric layer through the center opening to turn the assembly right side out, as shown in **Figure C**. Press carefully around the circular seam of the muslin frame.

2. Place the cross-stitched aida cloth right side up, and center the muslin frame over it. Baste the three layers together (**Figure D**). Carefully whipstitch the aida cloth to the muslin, taking tiny invisible stitches around the entire circular seam.

3. Cut a third 26-inch muslin square, and a matching square of bonded quilt batting. Place the plain muslin square on a flat surface. Stack the batting and then the aida and frame assembly on top (right side up). Baste the layers together, beginning at the center and working out to the four edges.

4. Enlarge the quilting pattern given in **Figure E** to full-size. Check to make certain that the quilting pattern will fall outside the cross-stitched center circle, and then transfer the pattern to the right side of the muslin frame using the special fabric marker. Place the work in the quilting hoop, adjusting it so that the fabric is smooth and even.

Figure F

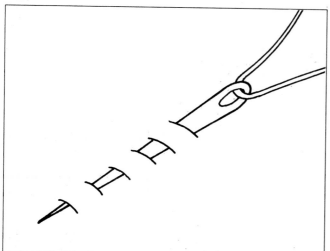

Figure G

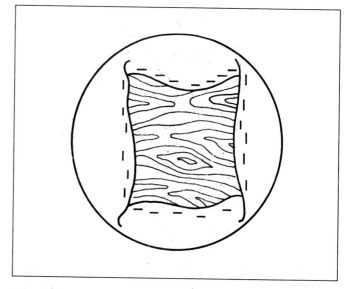

5. Quilt the design using quilting needle and thread. The quilting stitch used is a very even running stitch, approximately ⅛ inch long (**Figure F**).

6. Remove the work from the hoop, pull out the basting stitches, and press gently with a steam iron.

Attaching the chair seat

1. Cut three 16-inch-diameter circles of bonded quilt batting. Stack the three layers and center them over the 15-inch plywood circle. Center the quilted fabric seat on top of the batting and plywood.

2. Turn the entire assembly upside down, so the quilted fabric is flat against a work surface, and the plywood is on top. Pull the fabric edges taut and staple them to the plywood, stretching and smoothing the fabric as you work. Staple the fabric at opposite points on the circle first, and then at points midway between the first staples (**Figure G**). Check the front side of the assembly occasionally to make sure you have not pulled the design off center, and continue to staple at opposite points on the circle, between the previous staples.

3. Place the assembled seat on the chair, and turn the entire chair upside down so that the seat rests flat on the work surface. Attach the seat to the chair, inserting screws through the bottom. After inserting the first screw, check the position of the chair seat again, and then add the remaining screws.

Adding the trim

1. Encase the cotton cord in the wide bias binding. Stitch as close to the cording as possible, using a zipper foot attachment on your sewing machine (**Figure H**).

2. Glue the fabric-covered cord around the outer edge of the fabric seat, beginning and ending at the back. Tuck the raw edges between the chair seat and fabric (**Figure I**).

Figure H

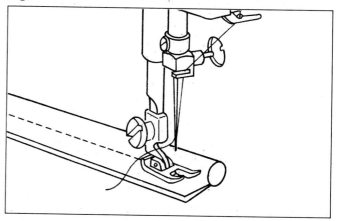

Figure I

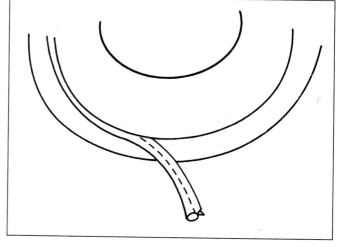

142

Folk Pillows

You can safely break house rules and allow this dog and cat to sleep peacefully on the couch or easy chair. They won't shed a single hair, and you never have to feed them!

Materials

13 x 18-inch piece of dark red calico print fabric.
13 x 18-inch piece of navy blue polka-dot fabric.
Two pieces of ivory-colored 14-count aida cloth, each 13 x 18 inches.
Embroidery floss in dark red and navy blue.
One large bag of polyester fiberfill.
Tapestry and regular needles, white thread, pins, scissors, pattern paper, sewing machine.

Cross-stitch

A cross-stitch graph for the sleeping cat is provided in **Figure A**, and for the dog in **Figure B**. The designs are worked using stitches that are twice as high and twice as wide as normal. Each complete cross-stitch covers four aida cloth squares, instead of covering only one square.

Home Decor

Solid outlines and broken seam lines for the cat and dog are included on the stitching graphs, so you can determine where to place the designs on the aida cloth. Work the cat design (but not the outline) in red on one piece of aida cloth. Work the dog design in blue on the remaining piece of aida cloth.

Assembling the pillows

Note: All seam allowances are ½ inch.

1. Use the cat outline provided in **Figure A** as a scale drawing for the cat pattern. Enlarge the drawing to full size, using a scale of 20 squares to one inch.

2. Place the paper pattern over the cross-stitched cat design on the aida cloth, refering to **Figure A** for placement, and cut the cloth to the shape of the pattern. Cut an additional cat from red calico, placing the pattern upside down on the right side of the fabric.

Figure B

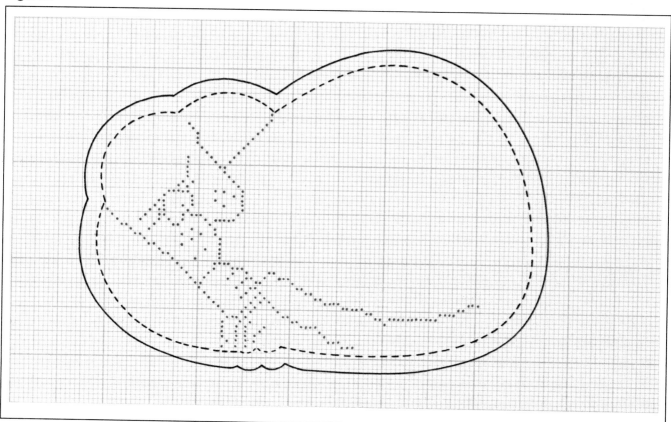

3. Pin the calico and aida cloth pieces right sides together and stitch the seam all the way around the outline, leaving a 4-inch opening at the bottom (**Figure C**). Clip the corners and curves, and turn the cat right side out. Use a pencil or other pointed object to turn the points of the ears completely.

4. Stuff the cat tightly with fiberfill. (Since aida cloth is made to retain its squareness, you'll find that the stuffed cat will not have very smooth curves unless you stuff it quite tightly, pushing and manipulating the stuffing until the curves loose their pointiness.) Whipstitch the opening edges together.

5. The cat has a calico bow for decoration. To make the bow, cut a piece of red calico 2¾ x 9 inches. Fold the fabric in half lengthwise, placing right sides together, and stitch a ¼-inch-wide seam across one short end and down the long edge (**Figure D**).

6. Turn the calico tube right side out and press a ¼-inch allowance to the inside on the remaining raw edges. Fold the strip into a loop, overlapping the ends by about 1½ inches. Wrap a length of thread around the center of the loop and pull it tight to form a bow.

7. Cut a piece of red calico ⅝ x 1 inch. Press a narrow hem allowance to the wrong side on each edge, and wrap the strip around the bow to cover the center thread (**Figure E**). Overlap and tack the ends at the back of the bow. Tack the bow to the cat pillow.

8. Assemble the sleeping dog pillow in the same manner, using the navy blue polka-dot fabric.

Figure C

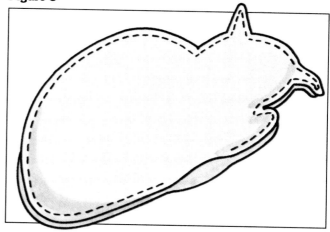

Figure D

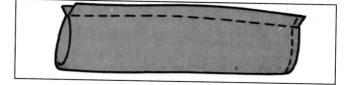

Figure E

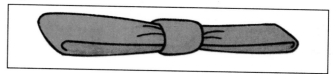

144

Kitchen Canisters

These oversized country canisters are built to accommodate full five-pound sacks of both sugar and flour. Your cross-stitch handiwork is protected by a glass cover on the front. (We have kids too!)

Materials

10 linear feet of ½ x 10-inch pine. If your lumberyard cannot supply this material, you can substitute an equivalent amount of ½-inch-thick lumber-core plywood.

Four wooden drawer knobs (two large and two small).

Four rectangles of ⅛-inch-thick glass; two 7 x 9 inches, and two 5½ x 7 inches.

Four rectangles of ivory-colored 14-count aida cloth; two 9½ x 11 inches, and two 8 x 10 inches.

Embroidery floss in brown, red, and gold.

Four rectangles of ⅛-inch-thick cardboard; two 7 x 9 inches, and two 5½ x 7 inches.

Tapestry needle, scissors, steam iron, hammer, small finishing nails, carpenter's wood glue, carpenter's square, saber saw, medium and fine grit sandpaper, nailset, wood filler, and wood stain.

A router or table saw is necessary to cut grooves in the frame pieces. If you do not have access to one of these tools, purchase 12 linear feet of ¼ x ¾-inch pine stock, and follow the instructions in the "Alternate frame construction."

Cross-stitch

A color-coded cross-stitch graph for the four canister fronts is given in **Figure A**. The rooster and hen should be worked in the center of the larger aida rectangles, and the chicks on the smaller rectangles. Press each piece gently on the wrong side using a steam setting.

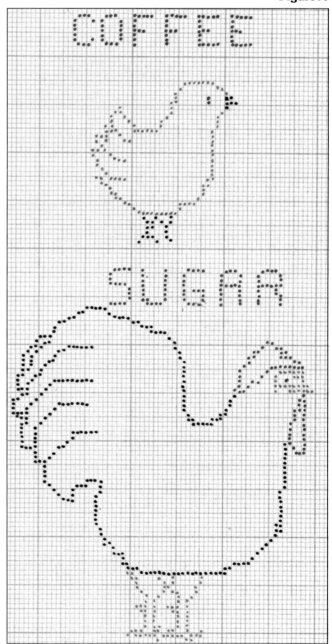

Home Decor

Figure A

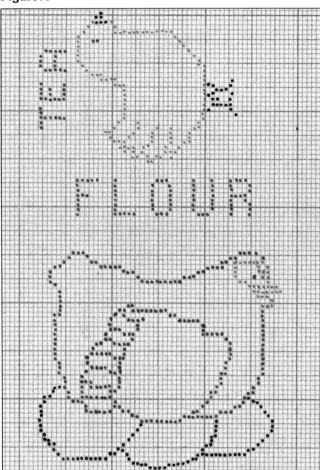

Figure B   1 square = 1 inch

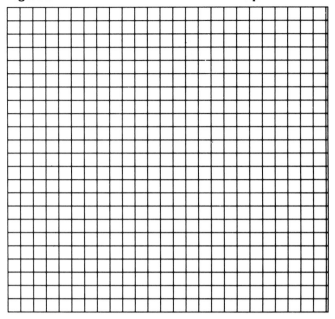

Figure C

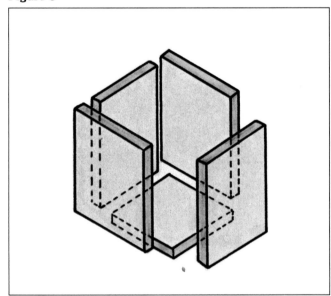

Figure D

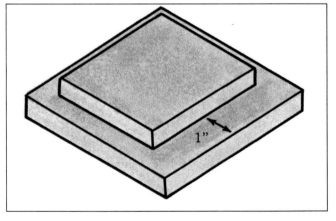

Building the large canisters

1. Scale drawings for the large flour and sugar canisters are given in **Figure B**. Enlarge the drawings to full size. For each canister, cut the following pieces from ½-inch wood stock: two sides, one front, one back, one bottom, one lid, and one inner lid.

2. Assemble the two sides, front, back, and bottom of the canister, butting the pieces as shown in **Figure C**. Glue and nail them together, recess the nails, and fill the holes with wood filler.

3. A diagram of the lid assembly is given in **Figure D**. Note that the inner lid is not centered, but is offset to accommodate the frame which will be added later to the front of the canister. Nail and glue the lid pieces together. Install the wood knob in the center, on top of the lid.

4. Repeat steps 2 and 3 above to assemble the remaining large canister.

Adding the frame

The frame pieces are grooved on the inner edges and attached to the front of the canisters to accommodate the glass and cross-stitch. If you do not have access to the tools needed to cut the grooves, alternative construction methods may be used and are described in the next section, "Alternate frame construction."

1 square = 1 inch   **Figure E**

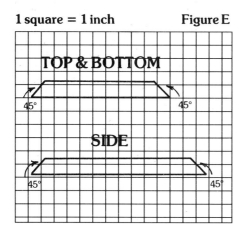

Figure F

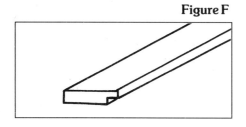

Figure G

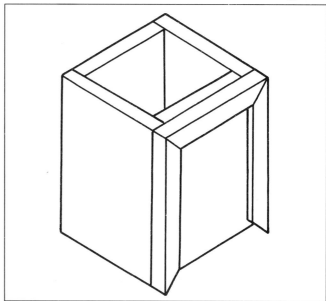

1 square = 1 inch   **Figure H**

(**Figure G**). Do not attach the bottom frame piece, but check to make sure that it will fit properly at the bottom of the frame, and will not extend below the bottom of the canister.

4. Sand the canister box, frame, and lid to eliminate splinters and rough surfaces.

5. Cut a piece of cardboard 7 x 9 inches. Sandwich the cross-stitched cloth between the cardboard and glass, centering the design, and trim off the excess cloth. Restack the cardboard, cross-stitch, and glass. Hold them together firmly, and insert them in the groove at the bottom, between the frame and canister.

6. Nail the bottom frame piece in place. It may be left unglued for easy removal of the cross-stitch if need be.

7. Repeat steps 3 through 6 to assemble the remaining large frame.

Alternate frame construction

1. If you are substituting ¼-inch wood, cut four frame pieces for each canister as shown in **Figure E**. Cut a duplicate set of frame pieces for each canister. Trim ¼ inch from the inner edge of each duplicate frame piece.

2. Glue the trimmed pieces to the corresponding untrimmed pieces, with outer edges flush. The pieces will now look like the routed frame piece shown in **Figure F**.

3. To complete the frame assembly, follow steps 3 through 7 in "Adding the frame".

Building the small canisters

Scale drawings for the small canister parts are provided in **Figure H**. Enlarge the drawings to full size. Cut the pieces and assemble the small canisters, following the same procedures described for the large canisters.

1. Scale drawings for the large frame pieces are given in **Figure E**. Enlarge the drawings to full size. For each large canister cut two side frames, one top frame and one bottom frame from ½-inch wood stock.

2. Cut or rout a ¼ x ¼-inch groove on the inner edge of each piece (**Figure F**) using a router or table saw.

3. Nail and glue the top and side frame pieces to the front of the assembled canister box, flush with the outer edges

Fireplace Match Holder

Your long fireplace matches will always be within reach in this attractive, easy-to-make holder. The entire project can be made from scraps of fabric, aida cloth, and embroidery floss to coordinate with your decor.

Materials

½ yard of medium-weight patterned fabric. We used a burnt orange fabric with a lighter orange pattern.

One piece of shirt cardboard, 5 x 18 inches.

1½ yards of ½-inch-diameter cotton cord.

Two 6-inch lengths of double-fold ¼-inch-wide bias tape.

4 x 6-inch piece of pale yellow 14-count aida cloth.

Embroidery floss in colors to coordinate with your fabric. We used orange and red.

Tapestry and regular needles, thread to match the patterned fabric, scissors, steam iron, and a sewing machine with a zipper foot attachment.

Figure A

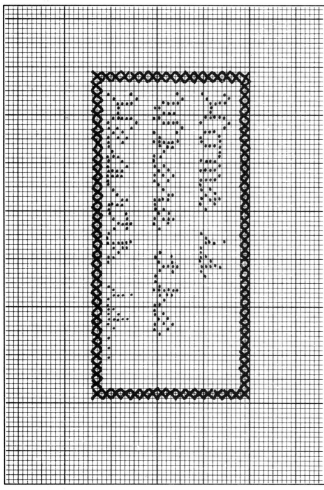

Figure B   1 square = 1 inch

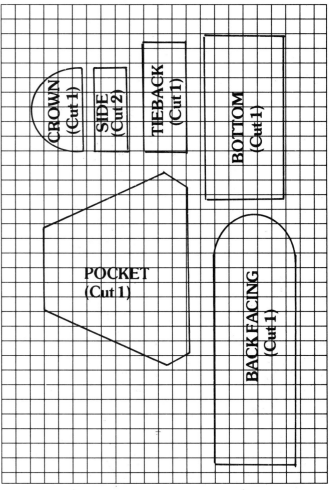

Home Decor

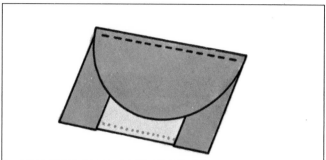

Figure C

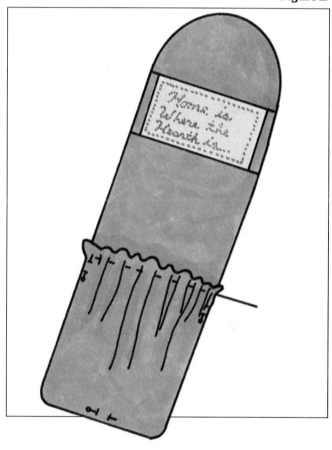

Cross-stitch

You'll find a cross-stitch graph for the message and border in **Figure A**. Stitch the design in the center of the aida cloth. We worked the first word of each line in red, the last word in orange, and the border in orange. Press the cloth gently, and trim it to 3⅝ x 5⅝ inches, keeping the borders even on all four sides.

Sewing the holder

Note: All seam allowances are ½ inch unless otherwise specified in the instructions.

1. Scale drawings for the holder pattern pieces are given in **Figure B**. Cut the following pieces from the patterned fabric: two sides, one crown, one bottom, one pocket, one tie-back, and one back facing.

2. Place the two side pieces right sides down on the aida cloth and stitch the side seams as shown in **Figure C**. Press the seams open.

3. Follow the same procedure to stitch the crown piece to the upper edge of the aida cloth (**Figure D**), and the bottom piece to the lower edge. Press the seams open.

4. Turn and press a ¼-inch hem allowance to the wrong side along the longer top edge of the pocket. Turn the same edge again, 1 inch deep, and stitch. Gather the top of the pocket just below the stitching line, using long basting stitches.

5. Pin the pocket (right side up) to the right side of the assembled front, with bottom and side edges even. Pull the gathering threads to form soft gathers across the top of the pocket as shown in **Figure E**.

Home Decor

Figure F

Figure G

Figure H

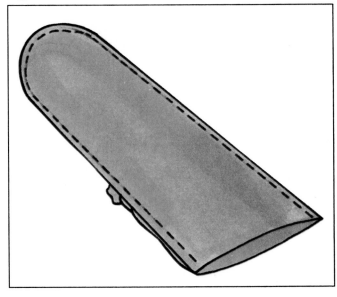

6. Fold the tieback piece in half lengthwise, placing right sides together, and stitch the seam along the long raw edges. Turn right side out and press.

7. Pin the tieback across the pocket gathers, so that the ends are even with the side edges of the pocket (**Figure F**). Stitch the pocket and tieback to the assembled front along the pocket seam line, beginning and ending at the upper corners of the pocket.

Adding the trim

1. Cut and piece together 2½-inch-wide bias strips of patterned fabric to form a continuous strip, 2½ x 54 inches.

2. Encase the cotton cord in the bias strip, folding the long raw edges of the fabric wrong sides together. Stitch as close as possible to the cord, through both fabric layers, using a zipper foot attachment.

3. Cut a 6⅛-inch length of the bias trim and place it across the assembled front section ½ inch above the aida cloth, so that the raw edges of the trim fabric are hidden. Pin the ends at the side seam lines.

4. Pin the remaining length of trim around the edges of the assembled front section (**Figure G**), so that the corded edge extends in toward the center. Begin and end at a lower corner, overlapping the ends, and cut off the excess. Baste the trim in place along the seam line.

5. Pin together the back facing and assembled front placing right sides together (the trim will be sandwiched between them) and stitch, leaving the straight lower edge open and unstitched (**Figure H**). Use a zipper foot, and stitch as close to the cord as possible. Clip the curves and turn the holder right side out. Press gently, turning the seam allowances to the inside on the open lower edges.

6. Use the assembled holder (minus the trim) as a pattern to cut a cardboard insert. Slip the cardboard insert between the fabric layers of the holder, and whipstitch the lower edges together.

7. Fold each of the 6-inch lengths of bias tape in half to form a loop. Whipstitch the ends of the loops to the back of the completed holder, spacing them about 3 inches apart and an equal distance from the top.

Welcome Ring

This cross-stitched welcome ring is a slight departure from the traditional door wreath. The frame is an 18-inch wooden embroidery hoop and the design includes a stuffed-fabric pineapple, complete with leaves and yarn spikes.

Materials

25 x 25-inch piece of white 14-count aida cloth.
¼ yard of tan-colored fabric, pre-quilted in a diamond design for the pineapple. (If you can't find anything close enough to pass for a pineapple, just purchase some quilt batting and twice as much un-quilted fabric in an appropriate color, and quilt it yourself.)
¾ yard of medium-weight green fabric, 45 inches wide.
1¾ yards of pre-gathered ruffling, 1½ inches wide. We used ruffling made from white cotton fabric with small green polka-dots.
1¾ yards of white blanket binding or wide double-folded seam binding.
2¼ yards of brown yarn.
Green embroidery floss.
18-inch wooden embroidery hoop.
Tapestry, embroidery, and regular sewing needles; sewing machine; pins; scissors; white, green, and tan thread; steam iron; pattern paper; and a glue gun with a small quantity of hot-melt glue (or substitute regular white glue).

Cross-stitch

An alphabet graph for the WELCOME message is provided in **Figure A**. Stitch the letters on the aida cloth, beginning with the "C." Place the lower edge of the "C" 4½ inches from the lower edge of the cloth, and equally distant from each side. Work the remaining letters diagonally above the "C" on each side, allowing ten blank vertical threads between each. The bottom of each letter should be even with the top of the letter below it.

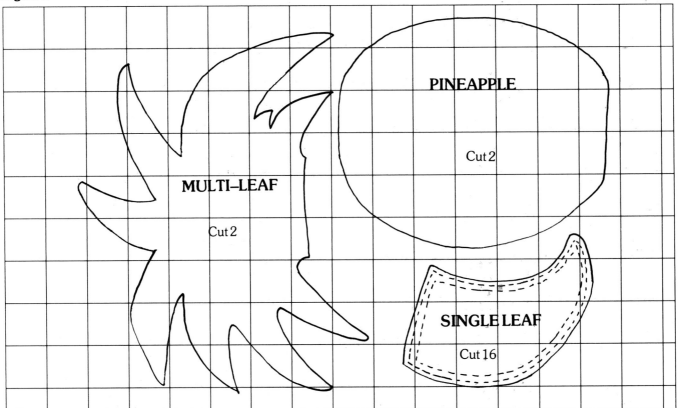

Making the pineapple parts

1. Scale drawings for the pineapple and two different leaf patterns are given in **Figure B**. Enlarge the drawings to full-size paper patterns.

2. Cut two pineapple pieces from the tan quilted fabric aligning the diamonds vertically. Pin the pieces right sides together and stitch the seam around the long curved edge, leaving the short straight edge open and unstitched (**Figure C**). Clip the curve and turn the pineapple right side out. Turn the remaining raw edges to the inside, and whipstitch the folded edges together.

3. Cut a 12 x 45-inch piece of the green fabric and set it aside for later use. Cut the leaves from the remaining green fabric, using the full-size patterns for the large multi-leaf piece and the smaller single leaf. Cut two fabric pieces using the large pattern, and sixteen pieces using the smaller pattern.

4. Pin the two large leaf pieces right sides together and stitch the seam around the contoured edges, leaving the short straight lower edge open and unstitched (**Figure D**). Clip the curves, and clip the corners all the way to the seam line so they won't wrinkle when turned right side out. Turn the stitched pieces right side out, using a pencil or similar object to turn the points.

5. Pin two of the single leaf pieces right sides together. Stitch, clip, and turn as you did the large leaf. Repeat these procedures, using the remaining single leaves two at a time, until you have made eight single leaves. Stitch six single leaves using a ¼-inch seam allowance, and two using a ½-inch allowance.

Figure C

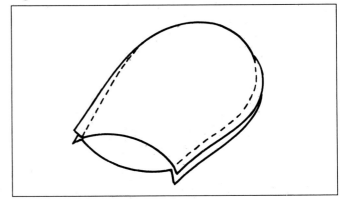

Figure D

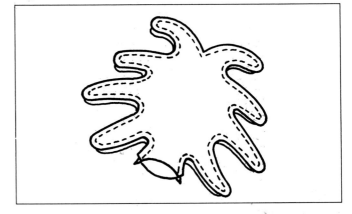

Figure E

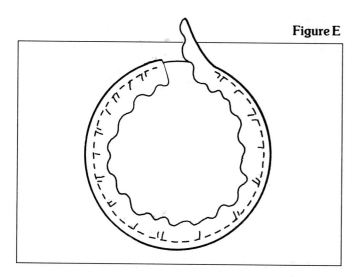

Figure F

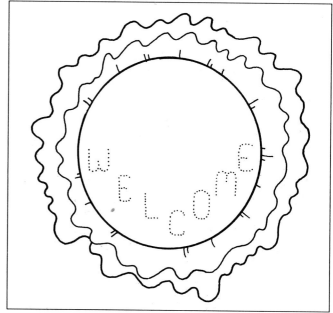

Figure G

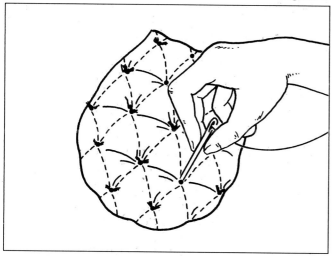

Assembly

1. Place the stitched aida cloth in the embroidery hoop so that the WELCOME is centered from side to side, and the lower edge of the "C" is 1 inch from the edge of the hoop. Use a pencil to mark a line on the cloth, all the way around the back of the hoop.

2. Remove the cloth from the hoop and place it right side up on a flat surface. Pin the bound edge of the pre-gathered ruffling to the right side of the cloth, ½ inch outside the pencil line (**Figure E**). The ruffled edge should extend in toward the center of the cloth. Begin and end at the top of the circle, overlapping the ends and turning the short raw edges to the wrong side. Baste the ruffle in place along the pencil line.

3. A second ruffle layer is made from the green fabric that you previously cut and put aside. Cut this piece in half lengthwise so that you have two strips, each 45 x 6 inches. Place them right sides together, stitch a seam across one short end, and press open. You should now have one continuous strip, 90 x 6 inches.

4. Fold the long green strip in half lengthwise, wrong sides together, and pin the long edges together. Run two lines of basting stitches along the long raw edges, one ¼ inch from the edges, and another ½ inch from the edges. Pull up the basting threads to form even gathers until the strip measures 60 inches long.

5. Follow the procedures described in step 2 to pin and baste the green ruffle over the polka-dot one. The raw edges of the green ruffle should be even with the bound edge of the polka-dot ruffle.

6. Now pin the blanket or seam binding over the ruffles in the same manner, so that one edge of the binding is even with the edges of the ruffles. Stitch through all thicknesses, ½ inch from the edges of the ruffles and binding. Turn the ruffles and binding outward and press (**Figure F**).

7. Replace the aida cloth in the embroidery hoop and tighten the screw securely. Trim away the excess aida cloth about 1 inch from the rear edge of the hoop. Fluff the ruffles forward, and glue the binding to the inside of the hoop.

8. Pin the pineapple to the aida cloth and tack it in place at the top and bottom. Tack through the aida cloth and the back of the pineapple only, so that the stitches do not show on the front.

9. Tie the pineapple to the aida cloth as you would tie a quilt, using brown yarn. To make a tie, thread the embroidery needle with brown yarn and take a stitch through both layers of the pineapple and the aida cloth, from front to back where any two lines of quilting stitches intersect (**Figure G**). Then take another stitch next to the first one, to return the needle and yarn to the front. Pull the yarn through and cut it off so that you have two even ends, each about 2 inches long. Tie them tightly in a square knot, and trim to approximately ⅜ inch. Make a tie at each quilting point.

10. Arrange and pin the large and small leaves to the aida cloth above the pineapple. When you have achieved an attractive arrangement, tack the leaves to the aida cloth and to each other, using hidden stitches.

Old-Fashioned Sampler

Cross-stitched samplers were one of the most popular forms of needlework in Early American days. They made lovely wall decorations, and mothers used them to teach their children the alphabet.

Materials

28 x 35-inch piece of ivory-colored 14-count aida cloth.
Embroidery floss in red, green, yellow, brown, and blue.
Tapestry needle, scissors, and a large embroidery hoop.
22 x 29-inch piece of interior grade ¼-inch-thick plywood.
Four lengths of standard 1 x 4-inch pine; two 35-inch lengths, and two 42-inch lengths.

Two small screw eyes and a 64-inch length of picture wire.
Staple gun with ¼-inch staples, wood glue, wood stain, varnish or sealer, hammer, several small tacks, and steam iron.
To make a frame like the one pictured here, you'll need the following additional tools: a router with dado bit, T-square, sandpaper, and wood chisel. A simpler frame can be made using only a saber saw and a miter gauge or miter box (see "Alternate frame construction").

Cross-stitch

A cross-stitch graph for the sampler is provided in **Figure A**. Because the sampler is so large, the graph is divided and spread over four pages. A color photograph of the intact sampler is provided on page 155. Refer to the photograph to determine which colors of floss to use as you work the designs on the aida cloth. We designed the center portion of this sampler to depict the individual members of our family. However, you may wish to alter the design to depict the members of your own family.

Press your finished work on the wrong side of the fabric, using a steam setting. Staystitch ½ inch from each edge, turn the raw edges to the wrong side along the staystitching, and press. Topstitch ⅜ inch from each folded edge.

Making the frame

1. Place the aida cloth over the piece of plywood, centering the cross-stitched design. Wrap the hemmed edges of the fabric to the back of the plywood and staple them down. Be sure that you do not pull the design off center as you work, and try to use a consistent amount of tension so the fabric will look smooth and even, not wavy, on the front.

2. The two shorter lengths of pine 1 x 4 will serve as the upper and lower frame pieces, and the longer lengths will serve as the side pieces. The frame is assembled using half-lap joints, as shown in **Figure B**. A half-lap joint is formed by interlocking grooves cut into each piece of wood. For the sampler frame you'll need to cut a ⅜-inch-deep by 3½-inch-wide groove near both ends of each frame piece. To determine exact placement of the grooves, place the upper and lower frame pieces on a flat surface, parallel to each other and 28¼ inches apart. Place the side frame pieces on top, parallel to each other and 21¼ inches apart, leaving equal extensions on all ends. Mark a guide line across each board where it is overlapped by another board. To cut each groove, you will need to make several passes across the board between the guide lines, using a router with a dado bit set to a depth of ⅜ inch.

3. Assemble the frame pieces, glue the joints, and allow them to dry thoroughly.

4. The sampler is set into a groove cut around the inner edge on the back of the assembled frame. Use a router with a dado bit to cut a ⅜ x ⅜-inch groove along all four back inner edges of the frame. Use the chisel to finish cutting the groove at the corners.

5. Sand, stain, and seal the assembled frame. When it is dry, insert the sampler into the routed back edge and secure using small tacks.

6. Insert a screw eye at each side on the back of the frame, and attach the picture wire between them.

Figure B

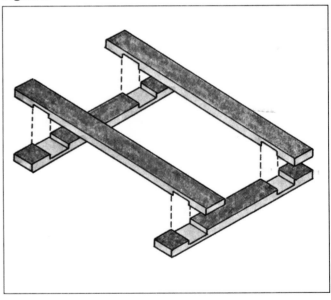

Alternate frame construction

A simple frame can be made by cutting and mitering the lengths of pine 1 x 4 to fit around the plywood. Miter both ends of each frame piece at a 45 degree angle and join the corners of the frame using glue and finishing nails. Secure the sampler inside the frame using small tacks inserted through the back at an angle.